MY SOUL SWIMS THE BOYNE

By Amanda Griffith

ISBN: 978-1-911131-67-0

This book was published in cooperation with
Choice Publishing, Drogheda, Co. Louth,
Republic of Ireland.
www.choicepublishing.ie

Cover Illustration. *Stackallan Bridge* taken from my father's favourite spot on the riverbank.

All stories are as my father recounted them, they are his memories and his recollections alone. Apologies if there are any inaccuracies but I have remained true to his word and regularly read the content back to him to make sure his stories were correct. All photographs have been taken from my father's personal collection.

In memory of a wonderful father, grandfather and brother
who placed his family at the heart of everything.

Contents

Foreword

My father, John Patrick Reilly was born and raised at Castlefin Lock, a tiny riverside cottage hidden deep in the woods on the outskirts of Slane, County Meath, Ireland. He was a quiet, principled man with an adventurous spirit and an exceptionally generous nature but above all, he was a dedicated family man who never forgot his humble beginnings. In 1949 when he was 22 years old he took a brave and courageous step into the unknown. Without any preconceived ideas about how long he would stay or what his future may look like he set sail to England to seek better work opportunities. After meeting my mother in 1950, he made the decision to remain in England where he lived for 67 years but he returned to Ireland for annual holidays, weddings and of course the occasional funeral. Throughout his life, he kept in close contact with his parents, all his brothers and sisters and many friends 'from home' and would like nothing better than sitting down for a long chat with each of them over the telephone in between visits. He kept the link and his ties to Slane and Ireland very strong, he was very proud of his family and all they had achieved and was particularly in awe of his mother Kitty, who he said was the hardest worker he had ever known. Even after leaving home and spending the majority of his years in England he managed to retain his fine Irish brogue, there was no mistaking where he was from and I loved him dearly for that; a softly spoken gentle giant from the 'The Free State', as he would often say, a fine figure of a man, with a mighty personality and heart of gold to match.

Although well read on the subject, he wasn't excessively political or wrapped up in the intricacies of Irish History but he was keen for his children to understand their heritage, to know and love the place where he was born, but more than anything he wanted for us to be a meaningful part of his extensive family on 'the other

1

side of the water'. We visited regularly from a young age, I still do and testament to the good job that my father did, I can safely say that I know many of my Irish cousins, as well as I know my English cousins! He has managed to instil in both my brother Damian and I what he wanted, a love of his homeland, a love of his family and a belonging to Ireland, something I feel particularly passionate about.

With his health failing, in 2014 he moved in to live with me and my family. Communicating with him was often difficult, he was totally deaf in one ear and had only partial hearing in the other and following a fall at home he not only endured a long and difficult stay in hospital recuperating from a fractured pelvis he also had to adjust to the devastating news that the recent and sudden onset of blindness that developed while he was there – was permanent. From being a very independent man all his life, everything changed very suddenly for him and of course, for my family too. He had rheumatoid arthritis, which he said he had inherited from his mother's side of the family and he endured pain in most of his joints, slowing him down considerably in latter years and if that wasn't enough to deal with, he also lived with Chronic Lymphocytic Leukaemia - a slow developing cancer! As his needs intensified and his need for help increased there were occasions when I doubted my ability as a carer but his unfailing positivity, optimism and enthusiasm

Silent prayers in my garden 2015

2

made him a joy to be around and before long my family and I referred to him as our very own Mr. Sunshine! I became his eyes and ears and I supported him in every capacity but I also worked hard at trying to make his days more interesting, more meaningful and more colourful. There were days when we couldn't leave the house, other days centered around hospital visits of one kind or another and a stretch into the garden was often as good as it got. I felt sad for all he had lost and there were days when I couldn't bear to see him just sat in his chair isolated with his own thoughts or just praying with his rosary in hand. To involve him in conversations, we all learned to speak slowly and loudly, he could no longer read, watch the television, or work in his beloved garden.

The speed of the events that stole his independence was shocking and we all struggled to adjust, so to make his days more interesting I suggested one day that we sit down and write down some of his favourite memories together. He had always been quite a raconteur and his memory seemed to be the only thing that was not failing him and so in between, motherhood, housework and my caring responsibilities we would sit down and chat. I would get my little table out, set up the computer and he'd talk and talk and talk while I typed as fast as I could. I pressed him for detail and made him repeat things over and over and in my quiet moments I would conduct my own research, reading maps, old newspaper stories and local history books and I would smile as he got excited whenever I re-read anything of interest back to him. Eventually we put together what he called 'his little book' and in his final days when he was bed bound and weary, I would sit by his side and read his own stories back to him. It was one sure way of bringing a smile to his face. Quite unexpectedly a couple of days before he died, he asked me to publish his stories, "They'll be of interest to someone, I'm sure" he said. I agreed of course, unaware of the challenge that I had set myself but I could see that this made him happy and as I read on I was glad that he couldn't see the tears in my eyes or hear my voice falter as his own words took him back to the place that I know he loved best of all. It was a poignant moment for me when I realised that his life had in a sense come full circle.

So here they are, my father's favourite memories, and even though I set off on our little journey together intending 'his little book' to be his life story from start to finish, it soon became clear that that would never happen - time was simply not on our side. It also soon became clear that he only ever really wanted to talk about his upbringing, his boyhood days, life as a young man and his Irish roots. He was good at changing the topic and bringing us back to the stories he loved best, the stories he only really wanted to tell, the stories of life around the River Boyne. This rich fast flowing and spectacular river, his river, was in his blood, was in his heart and undoubtedly within his soul.

Enjoy.

1

The Early Years

As a boy, I never realised that I was growing up in a part of the world steeped in so much fascinating history and although I was made more aware of the importance of the area as a teenager, I didn't learn about the true historical value of my surroundings until much later on in life.

Three miles north of where I was born lies the Hill of Slane, where St. Patrick allegedly lit a paschal fire in defiance of the pagan kings at Tara. Seven miles east is Newgrange, the prehistoric monument that is now a World Heritage site and a mile or two further along to the coast is Oldbridge, the site of the infamous 1690 Battle of the Boyne, which took place between King William of Orange and James II the deposed English Catholic King, the battle that forged Irish history. Much closer to home there is Slane Castle, home of The Conynghams, and on the opposite end of the spectrum the cottage of Francis Ledwidge, our local hero who was killed fighting in World War I.

Francis is now a celebrated poet and even though I didn't know him, I remember learning about him at school. I knew more of his brother Joseph and knew Joseph's two sons very well as they were about my age. Joseph was a clerk at the courts in Navan and a familiar sight pedalling off to work on his bike every morning wearing his suit, brown kid gloves and flat cap. He was quite a spectacle and everyone remarked on his unique style. Navan was about seven miles away from Slane Village and it was a steep climb in some parts for a man on a bike. I know this because I peddled that same route many times when I was older and working out at Gerrity's furniture factory there. It was a lovely ride when the weather was fine and the wind was behind my back but boy I struggled when the rain pelted down and hit me hard in the face! It didn't half sting! Everyone remarked that Joseph must have had a strong constitution as he never, ever wore an overcoat or seemed to feel the cold regardless of the weather and despite having the bike, he was also one of the few in the village to own a car. He rarely used his car as he preferred to cycle and I seem to recall that his registration number was 'A1' - nowadays it would probably be worth a fortune. The Ledwidge family cottage is now a museum on the outskirts of the village and is a perfect example of the way we all lived back then.

Despite the historical importance of the area, I knew nothing of this as a boy. For the first seven years of my life, all I knew was a five or six mile stretch along the lush, green Boyne Valley and the spectacular scenery of the area. The endless expanse of trees, majestic ones, short and misshapen ones, prickly pines standing tall and, on some days, the colours were truly breath-taking. These wooded vales and streams that stretched beyond the back of the house were my playground and where I spent all my time in those early years. I had no idea of the world beyond and life was as simple as it gets. In the summer, there were glades of bright green grass to play in, wild strawberries to pick and eat to my heart's content and there were times when I would just sit on the riverbank and watch the river sparkle in the sunlight. As I grew a little older I learned to recognise the heights of the beech, elm, larch, hazel, lime and chestnut trees, and spent hours clambering through the laurels, sweet-briars, thorns and quite often the nettles of the riverbank. The uneven ground was forever green and I loved the feel of the dew under my bare feet in the early morning hours. Certain trees and shrubs marked my boundaries and I never defied my parents by going beyond them. I had been warned of the dangers of living on the riverbank from an early age.

The tranquility of the river valley was often captivating and the colours mesmerising, especially in the autumnal months when to me the valley bloomed in all its majestic and sometimes mystical glory. In the summer months the sound of the waters cascading over the weirs was really soothing and I found it easy to relax by the water's edge. When calm, the river was mirror-like in places and there were shallow spots here and there that I got to know well. As a boy, I would often lie on my stomach on the grassy bank and hang my head over the edge to stare at my reflection in the water. I would pull faces at myself and laugh at my unkempt appearance, my hair sticking up or my crumpled shirt and I would sink my fingers into the cold water to pick at anything I could find. I loved to make ripples and watch them spread slowly across the surface and I could linger for a long time simply making patterns in the water. There were times however when the River Boyne looked evil too. The water was deep in places and could appear as black as coal, especially in the shaded wooded areas where the long tree branches would overhang the water. When the river was swollen and the river raged, I was terrified as a child of being too close to the water's edge and never had to be reminded to keep my distance. The winter months were always different, the landscape and colours of the trees changed as many lost their leaves, it appeared quieter and my adventures were somewhat curtailed too as I was confined to the house to play in front of the fire where it was cosy and warm.

Life now, 89 years later is hugely different. I live in a very modern world and I am in awe of the technology and information that my children and grandchildren have at their fingertips. With laptop in hand and the quick flick of a switch they can instantly learn and explore the world from the comfort of an armchair - what luxuries. Despite our different experiences of growing up, I do firmly believe that my life has been far richer than any one of them will ever appreciate but now hampered by rheumatoid arthritis, leukaemia, blindness and partial deafness, it is too late for me to embrace the world of computers. Sadly, I no longer live independently and following a nasty fall in 2014, I now live with my daughter Amanda and her small family. I have all the comforts of a modern family home, I am well cared for and want for nothing but there is a sense of isolation within me that I can't shake off. Recognising this and to help with my rehabilitation, Amanda suggested we work together on compiling my memoirs and so every day without fail, we sit and work together on my 'little project'. It brings me immense joy, provides a reason for living as well as great delight that others may be interested in my stories.

All the information in this book is therefore based on my own recollections and I genuinely believe them to be factually correct. Apologies to anyone if some of my facts are confused but in reality I doubt that they will be, as my memory serves me well, it's all I have! Answering Amanda's questions and immersing myself in this work, has not only caused me to have many colourful dreams about old friends and old times that I have never forgotten, but it has also transported me back to those wonderful innocent days and a time that I want future generations of my family to understand and be proud of. I believe that my humble beginnings have served me well and I hope the family values, life lessons and skills I have picked up and shared along the way will help keep my family grounded, as well as good moral members' of any society they live amongst. Unfortunately, my dreadfully poor eyesight means that I will never be able to see my completed works but I have corrected and added to facts as Amanda has read them aloud to me. It has taken some time and I have enjoyed every single minute and to her, I will always be eternally grateful. For her commitment to her Irish heritage, I have given her the shillelagh that my father gave to me many years ago and my mother's irons that I watched her use so many times. I hope they will continue to serve as a reminder of that simple life that was innocent and carefree and I hope that she will cherish them as much as I have.

I was born not far from Slane Village, in a tiny cottage on the north bank of the River Boyne, Co. Meath, Ireland. It was an unusual little place and the cottage itself straddled a small tributary of the rich dark Boyne waters that ran approximately 30 yards from our front door. Sandwiched between our house and the main river were the canal ramparts and Loc Chaisléan na Finne or Castlefin Lock, one of the 20 locks built as part of the Boyne Navigation. Work on this project commenced in 1748 and reading a few small books and articles on the subject, I know it was never a very successful venture but in 1901 the Irish census shows my grandfather, also John Reilly, as one of the lock-keepers. He was 60 years old and river traffic would have been much reduced from its more successful days, when the lighters would transport flour from Navan and the many mills in the area down river to the sea and port at Drogheda. He would no doubt have earned a small wage from the Inland Waterways and Navigation Company, the company charged with building the canal, but this would have been many years before I was born and when the canal project was deemed a viable proposition.

The locality was known as Cruicetown, near Stackallan but in reality there was only a few buildings dotted here and there and everyone just referred to where we lived as 'Reilly's Place'. I'm not quite sure how our family first came to live in that house on the riverbank either and some locals say that it was initially built as a woodcutter's lodge deep in the Slane Castle Demesne where the Boyne Canal lock gates were actually made before it became a lock keeper's cottage, but I am not really sure. Even when I lived there between 1927 and 1934, it was only really accessible by boat or via the footpath along the canal ramparts, which in those days were a well-trodden and well-kept footpath. There was a lane on higher ground at the back of the house that led up to Wicker's Cross and Stackallan but to get to that you had to scramble through the woods and I was never allowed to do that. Stories in the family, passed down by previous generations, suggest that the first Reillys that lived there were evicted from their farm, which once occupied a site up by the current Roman Catholic Cemetery in the shadows of The Hill of Slane but I suspect that this will have been several generations before. Maybe my great-grandparents, William and Mary Reilly, were lock-keepers too but I will never know as records for that time have proved difficult to find, if they ever existed in the

Family grave at Monknewton Cemetery

first place. The deaths of my great-grandparents occurred in the aftermath of the Great Potato Famine which killed a large portion of the Irish population, and with suffering vast and food scarce many families not only encountered death and starvation but evictions from farms and property if they did survive. I will never know the true impact of the famine on my immediate family but the rumour that my ancestors were evicted is potentially correct considering the circumstances. What I do know about previous generations however, is that my great-grandparents,

William and Mary Reilly, are buried up at Monknewton Cemetery, with my own grandparents, John and Elizabeth Reilly, and several other family members. The headstone was erected and paid for by my grandfather's older brother William who sent money home from America for a memorial, and I often wonder if the stonemason was unable to read William's hand-writing, which may account for some of the spelling mistakes! Alongside them is my Uncle Christie's grave and I remember my father being furious when he found out that Christie had taken part of the family plot to bury his wife Josephine there in 1957. My father had always wanted the plot for himself but it was all soon brushed over and Christie forgiven. Further hearsay suggests a child born within the family but not christened a Catholic was also buried between the two consecrated graves by my grandmother Eliza Reilly.

My grandfather John was born around 1841 and therefore he was just seven years old when his father William died and sadly eight years old when his mother Mary died the following year. I think to be orphaned at such a young age would have been tragic, but he did however have older siblings who were of a working age and I can only surmise that they all looked out for each other. Alternatively, maybe he was taken in by an aunt or an uncle until he was of an age to work, surely he didn't have to fend for himself when so young? Public records are scant and there are no family stories of orphanages or workhouses so I can only imagine he was cared for by older members of the family. Unfortunately extensive research through local records and ancestry websites hasn't uncovered the truth about the early years of my grandfather's generation so historically this is all rather vague and sadly it is unlikely that I will ever know the truth about how my life came to begin in that tiny lock keeper's cottage. Sadly I also do not have any photographs of my grandfather John Reilly, but I have unearthed some of my grandfather's brothers and wider family members and am taken aback by the strong family resemblance between the men in the family.

Life in rural Ireland would have been a lot more basic and a lot more difficult for my grandfather and his family, they grew up in desperate times. Baptismal records for Slane only commence in 1851 but from speaking to family members across the globe, I have established that my Grandfather John Reilly had three brothers, James who was born in 1836, William who was born in 1840, Matthew born in 1843, and that he also had a sister Mary who was born in 1845. There was potentially another sister called Maggie but I have yet to find any trace of her. Complicating my search further is the fact that I don't know exactly which townland or parish they lived in or came from and although I have always concentrated my efforts directly on the Slane area, the parishes of Rathkenny, Beauparc, Donore, Johnstown and Monknewton are significant within the family. In addition our surname can be spelt in many forms - Reilly, Riley, Rielly, Reilley, O'Reilly and even the Gaelic Ó Raghallaigh appears on many documents so I think the detail will always remain a mystery.

I do know however, that my grandfather's uncles emigrated to America (mainly via Canada), in the mid to late 19th century, eventually settling in Cleveland, Ohio. To my great joy, Amanda has traced ancestors and in 1993 I travelled to America for the first time with my wife Rita to visit Mary Nemec, granddaughter of James Reilly and my second cousin. Mary is two years older than I and from the moment we met, we gelled immediately. We continue to swap letters, cards, photographs and share family news periodically, which I find remarkable and on that visit I listened with great interest as Mary shared her own perspective of our family heritage. We are both saddened that neither of us have been able to unearth any formal document that categorically links the two families but our shared stories cannot be a coincidence and that is proof enough for me. It is reputed that my grandparents John and Elizabeth Reilly (née O'Neil) travelled out to America to join the rest of this family at some juncture but preferred the life they left behind and returned to Slane where they finally set up home. This may be true or maybe they were too frail and refused entry as so many emigrants were but regardless, I have not found any evidence of their travels. To add to the mystery further John and Elizabeth's eldest son William,

as detailed on his American naturalisation papers, was born in Darlington, England in 1873 and once more, I am not sure how this came to be. In 1889, he was invited to America by his Uncle Matthew who had written to tell him about the work opportunities out there and by all accounts he didn't hesitate to move on. If only I could turn back time and speak to my father about it all now.

Elizabeth Reilly nee O'Neil
1851-1928

John's wife, my grandmother Elizabeth, reputably gave birth to 22 children. My father Richard, who was born in 1900, was the second youngest in the family and the last to leave home. When he married my mother on 9th November 1927, instead of setting up a new home with his bride like all his brothers and sisters had done, he took my mother back to that small and isolated cottage on the riverbank, where he lived with his own mother and as a consequence it became the first place that I ever called home. I think back and wonder in amazement how anyone could bring up so many children in a house so small but in reality, only 14 of her children survived infancy and as with the generation before, some left for both America and England to search for work, whilst others moved further along the river to live in a separate lock keeper's cottage at Cruicetown, making room in the original family home for younger members of the family (confirmed via the 1911 census). There was 27 years between my father Richard and his eldest brother William (born 1873) and both the times and the difficult conditions they were raised in guaranteed that they never knew each other, other than through correspondence.

With my grandmother having had so many children, my family tree is exceptionally complex and still incomplete despite copious amounts of research. As a child I remember a big purple velvet photograph album at the house which had many photographs of old relations and I would often sit and look through it with my mother. All the men seemed to have big thick moustaches and wore high stiff collars, they all seemed well dressed and I wish I knew who they all were. Sadly the album has gone missing and even though I have asked all my family with regard to its whereabouts no one seems to know what happened to it, which is such a shame. How I would love to have that book now and study those pictures once more and understand how we all knit together. Instead, I have reproduced some of what I know at the back of this book about my family history, should it be of any interest to anyone.

The circumstances of my own birth are also shrouded in an element of mystery and of course I never felt obliged to discuss them with anyone once I discovered that I was born only the day after my parents married. It was a great shock to me when I found this out when looking through church records some 60 years later and I was very uncomfortable with my discovery. I was part of a devout Catholic family and I felt an element of shame. My father had long since died and my mother was old and frail, it was not appropriate to delve into this part of their past so although I would have dearly loved to have understood more about why this was, I left well alone and did not ask any questions.

My father was eight years older than my mother and I often wondered when and where they met. Was it at school, or church or even a dance. There were a lot of outdoor kitchen dances around that time where neighbours would meet and socialise so maybe it was at one of those? Why did they leave it so late to get married? Was that my mother's or my father's decision? Did my Grandfather Harding even have some say in the matter? I've even thought about my mother getting to the church from McGruder's Cross whilst heavily pregnant and have come to the conclusion that perhaps Grandfather Harding took her there in his pony and trap. Such curiosity.

I was born in the winter of 1927 when my mother was only 18 years old and although my grandmother was 76 at the time, she is likely to have helped with my birth. There wouldn't have been any pain relief or qualified nurses in attendance but in those days ladies of the community helped each other during labour. It must have been quite frightening for my mother, especially in such primitive conditions and even if my grandmother could only offer words of comfort and encouragement, I'd like to think my mother's friends or even her sisters came to help as best they could - providing they knew of course that things were underway! My mother told me years later that this grandmother loved to cradle me and she would often tease me that my Granny Reilly 'nursed me soft'. I don't remember her at all as she died five months after I was born but I daresay she would have been a great help to my mother who was new to motherhood.

I was christened John Patrick. John after my paternal grandfather who had died in 1908 and Patrick after my maternal grandfather who I remember as being a very gentle and quiet old man. He was always smartly dressed, he had a big moustache and a full head of thick white hair. Although he only lived a couple of miles away, I didn't see him or any of my mother's brothers or sisters while we lived at Castlefin and only came to know them once we moved up to the new house in the lane at Cruicetown, when I was seven years old. I loved visiting him and I would often go up to my grandparent's house at McGruder's Cross in the evening after school. It was a five mile walk from home and even though I was only 11 or 12, the distance didn't bother me and of course in those days we were able to roam freely without fear. Grandfather Harding would take me out into his garden, he'd tell me about his plants and vegetables, about all the jobs he was doing and why he was doing them. Maybe this is where my love for being self-sufficient and 'living off the land' came from, as later on in my own life, I took great delight in gardening and growing my own produce, like both my father and grandfather before me.

The nearest village to our house on the River Boyne was called Slane and even though it was only approximately two miles downstream, I didn't go there until I was ten years old and I knew very little about life there until I was much older. My life for the early years was contained to the riverbanks, playing in the woods and running wild with my sisters Betty and Delia and of course my brother Liam who was only a toddler when we lived by The Boyne. Betty had actually been christened Alice Elizabeth so I understood her being called Betty but Delia had been christened Catherine, a name I never ever called her or heard her being called. When I asked why that was, years later I was told that when she was born she cried and cried and cried, creating havoc in the tiny house. My father, probably influenced by the lack of sleep, eventually said "Mammy, if we don't change that child's name, she'll cry forever - you better think of something else." After a few name changes, she

16

finally stopped crying when they called her Delia, so Delia she became!

When I reflect, I am the only one still called by his given name, although saying that I was called Sean by the headmaster at school on many occasions. My brother Liam was actually christened Richard William, my sister Maureen who was only ever a babe in arms whilst living at Castlefin, was christened Elizabeth Mary and my two younger brothers Patsy and Seamus, or Rusty to many, were christened Patrick Joseph and James respectively. We all carry names of grandparents and parents, names passed down from one generation to the next.

Betty, Mammy, Maureen on her knee, Liam, Me and Delia
c1933 in Hamill's Farmyard

The picture above was taken in Hamill's farmyard sometime around 1933 and is the only one of me as a child. I would be five or six years old. I spent many happy hours working in Hamill's yard when I was a teenager but every time I look at this photograph I think of the happy days down by the River Boyne. It captures us all at around the ages we were when we left there - the age of innocence for us all.

Top left: The Boyne tributary that runs through the woods and eventually under Castlefin lock keepers cottage.
Bottom left: Castlefin ruins with stream underneath and The Ramparts infront heading towards Slane Bridge.

Top Right: The boat house and tunnel under the ramparts, which leads out to the River Boyne. This area was always out of bounds to us children.
Bottom Right: Where the Boyne Canal meets the River Boyne in front of Castlefin. My father's allotment was on the centre island, was the length of the canal and accessible by walking along the top of the lock gates.

We would chase each other through the woods and wander through the trees for hours on end. There were few boundaries and although we lived dangerously close to the River Boyne and several deep canals, we were allowed to cross the 'gangplank' over the stream behind the house and go into the woods and play. The 'gangplank' was just an old piece of wood that my father had placed so that we could go beyond the stream without always getting our feet wet. It was in the opposite direction to the small boat house where we kept my father's fishing boat, and where my uncle Tom and other visitors would tie up their boats when they came by. It always had water inside, fed by both the river and stream, and I used to love sailing underneath the small arch with my father into the open waters of the main river. I was only allowed to do this in his charge and only when the Boyne waters were as still and as calm as they could be. It was a dangerous river and my mother must have been at her wits end bringing up her small family there. It certainly would not be deemed safe for anyone in this day and age. A family tragedy from 1919 served as a reminder of the dangers, as my cousin Thomas Grace drowned in a neighbouring lock when only nine years old. The event was reported in the local newspaper and recounts the circumstance of the event as provided by my grandmother Elizabeth Reilly. My other cousin John Reilly who lived downstream from me and who was playing with Tommy at the time also gave evidence. I remember walking along the riverbank with my father when I was about six or seven years old and we came across a steel cross in the ground. I asked him why it was there and he just said he would explain when I was a little older. I never thought to question him further and we walked on. For whatever reason, he never did explain things to me but I learned that this cross marked the spot where Thomas Grace perished. I guess he didn't think I was old enough to understand when I first asked him about it.

LITTLE BOY DROWNED IN CANAL

On Monday last, Dr. J Branagar, Coroner for North Meath, held an inquest at Cruicetown, Stackallan, concerning the death of a little boy, named Thomas Grace, aged nine years. A jury was sworn of which Mr. Andrew Finnegan was the foreman. The first witness examined was Mrs. Elizabeth Reilly, who stated she was grandmother to the little fellow. His mother was dead and his father was in the army. About half past one she last saw him, and he was then in his usual good health. He went down the canal bank with his cousin, John Reilly. About three o'clock John Reilly came to her crying and told her that "Tommy" was drowned in Maguire's lock. "I went to the place." witness narrated, "and took a drag to search for the body. I saw his cap in the water. I sent for assistance and Edward Reilly was the first to come. He used the drag and brought the body to the surface. Murray Connor came on the scene and helped to carry deceased home. The boy, the cousin of the deceased was next examined. He was aged about nine years and was not sworn. While making a statement he appeared in a frightened condition and was crying at times. Relating how the fatality occurred he said that deceased had a fishing rod behind Maguire's house on the lock. He was casting in the line when he fell into the water. He went down twice and came up again each time. On coming to the surface the second time he caught hold of the sluice rod, which he held for about three minutes. He said to go for Johnnie Hamill as he was afraid to send home. Johnnie Hamill lived a half mile away, and his own house was only about three hundred yards from the lock. Just before he sank the third time he said "I will peg off my cap the way they will know where I am. I cannot stay here. I so going. I am getting perished." the little lad, it would appear, was then only holding on to the sluice rod with his fingers, as it would be impossible to get a firm hold of the sluice rod from the position he was in. As he sank in the water bubbles came to the top. "I ran," continued the little witness, "and told his grandmother what had happened." the spot where the drowning took place was only four feet from the top of the bank, and with some assistance the little chap's life might have been saved. had the water been two feet higher he would have been able to catch the top of the bank. Dr. J.P. Sheridan, M.O., Wilkinstown in his evidence stated he examined the body and found that it showed no signs of bruises. Death was due to asphyxia caused by drowning. The jury returned a verdict in accordance with the medical evidence.

Extract reporting the death of Thomas Grace taken from
Meath Chronicle dated 1.3.1919

Life back then was just day after day of continuous play. We didn't have a care in the world and in reality, there was nothing else to do. I remember with fondness one time when Betty and I wandered to the quarry where they'd dug the stones out to build the canal, it was a safe area to play and it was all overgrown with flowers and wild strawberries. We stopped and feasted on the strawberries until we couldn't eat any more, it was a lovely sunny day and it is one of my all-time favourite memories of life down there.

We never had to be home for any set time and we were generally free to come and go as we pleased although we always knew never to roam too far. My mother never seemed to mind as she was always preoccupied with a new baby and I guess it was easier for her if we took ourselves off from under her feet and occupied ourselves somewhere else. We never had much by way of toys, we didn't even have a ball, we just had each other for company. It was an honest and respectable upbringing all considered - full of imaginings and to me, life was one long adventure playing games of my own making.

When Delia and Liam were old enough to play with us it was even better and on one particular occasion I remember that Delia found an old barrow, placed Liam inside and proceeded to push him around everywhere. Liam was only a toddler and he was giggling and laughing, enjoying the ride but Delia must have got tired as they both fell over into the small stream and were both drenched. Liam ended up cutting his nose quite badly and the laughter was soon replaced by howls and tears. My father had to go and get the doctor too as the bleeding wouldn't stop and due to our remote location that would have taken some considerable time. That was quite an eventful day.

We would play for hours out in those woods and in particular under the huge elm tree where the goats gathered. When it rained we sheltered there as it always stayed dry but the goats sheltered there too and they smelled awful so we never lingered there for too long. We'd kept goats since Delia was a baby, ever since the Doctor came to visit us when she was poorly. As a young one she was often sick and the doctor said things would only improve if she had goat's milk. I suspect she was allergic to mother's milk and cow's milk and that's why she cried so much when she was first born! We had one black goat and three black and white ones and my mother would milk them twice a day. They were always chewing the grass around the house and therefore she never had to round them up, they would all just wander up to the front door to be milked when they were ready and when the task was done, they would take themselves off to chew more grass until the next milking time. My family had always kept goats and the Petty Sessions Order books from 1884 confirm this, as my grandfather John Reilly was fined 1d with additional costs of 1/6d in April for allowing three of his goats to trespass in Boyne Wood, the property of Slane Castle. In May when it happened again, his fine was increased to 2/- with costs 1/6d, a heavier fine it seems for a repeat offender! I was quite amused to find this out as it brings my family to life more, especially as I can imagine the surroundings - I knew the Boyne Woods very well. As my grandfather had kept goats, I imagine that's why my own father kept goats, family tradition I guess but also because they'd be fairly cheap to keep and easy to manage. They roamed everywhere, we didn't have any fancy shelter for them so overall we got good returns from them for minimal effort. My mother would use the goat's milk in the dough of her soda bread and I would always stay close to the house when I saw her milking the goats and then making the morning bread. The warm crust spread with butter and homemade damson jam was a firm favourite of mine and I was generally first in line when it was ready.

Whilst playing, we would also spend hours looking for birds' nests, to see if we could see birds sitting on them and of course see if there were any eggs. From an early age we could identify birds from the sounds they made and the likes of water coot, water hen, swans, ducks, blackbirds, thrushes and robins were all familiar to me. Despite us rummaging and searching for nests, it was drummed into us that we should never take any eggs if we found any - and of course, we never did. I climbed thousands of trees, an elm tree and a particular ash tree were my favourites, and I could be found many a time swinging on the branches. About 30 yards away from the house, there was a large larch tree but I couldn't climb this one as there were no branches low enough to the ground to climb up onto. It produced a little bud that smelled lovely and one day I remember putting a bud up my nose because I thought it smelt so nice. Needless to say, it got stuck and it was there three days before I sneezed it out.

2
Chaisléan na Finne
(*Castlefin*)

There is no doubt that the first house I ever lived in was nestled in the most beautiful and often breathtaking of surroundings. It was however far from practical. It was exceptionally small and exceedingly basic. It was only about 12ft. square which is unimaginable in this day and age but to me it was all I knew and it was home. There was no mains gas or electricity or taps for running water, no carpets and few home comforts but at the heart of the house was the fireplace and the open hearth. We burned wood, collected from the woods by my father. We were all too small to make any worthwhile contribution to the chores so my parents would do everything and as a consequence they were always busy. Once cut, the wood was stored next to the hearth and my mother

Sketch of Castlefin Lock by my daughter Amanda

would ensure that the fire burned as long as necessary.

It was a traditional Irish whitewashed stone house with a slate roof, a single chimney, stone floor and a green front door that could split in half and to my recollection the top part was generally always open. Because we lived so close to the riverbank, there were numerous locks on the door to stop us getting out, the main one being far out of reach and on the outside. There were only two small windows, one on each of the side walls of the house but it wasn't dark as there was a permanent glow from the fire. To enhance the light in the evening we had plenty of candles and candle sticks but we also had one paraffin lamp which was very precious to my mother. My mother would wash the lamp's globe every day because it would blacken when the oil was burning and she would shout at us all if we went anywhere near it, "Keep away, you'll break my globe," she would cry. She must have loved that lamp, either that or it was a very expensive item!

The cottage was whitewashed on the inside too except for around the fireplace, which was blackened from the smoke from the fire and as we burned timber from the woods outside the smell from the fire was always delightful. Directly under the window to the left of the fireplace, my mother kept the settle bed, which was used as a seat during the day and opened up to become the bed where me and my sisters slept at night. As soon as it went dark, we'd get homemade biscuits and hot milk and while we enjoyed our supper, my mother would pull the settle bed out and we would all crawl into bed altogether. The girls would lie at the top and I would lie at the bottom and after Liam was born, he would be lifted in by my mother and lay beside me. We couldn't fall out because the sides were high but it got more and more cramped as the family grew. The mattress and pillows, which were stored inside the settle bed when it was a seat, were basic sacks of chaff gathered from the thrashing machines from the surrounding farms.

Every year the mattress was emptied out and refilled with fresh chaff and my parents would do this job together. I remember my mother sitting on a chair in front of the fire sewing the ends of the mattresses after they had been stuffed but despite all her efforts, the bed I slept on was far from comfortable, in fact, it was just like sleeping on the floor.

Opposite the settle bed, there was a wooden panel that had a door in it - the wooden panel stretched from the fireplace to the front door and my parents slept on the other side of the panel. When the girls got bigger, the girls went in there with my parents, while me and Liam stayed in the settle bed. My parents had a proper bed with a huge iron bed frame whilst Betty and Delia slept on a smaller bed at the foot of the big bed. I can't remember there being a chest for clothes but we didn't have many clothes other than the ones we wore so there really wasn't any need. There was no toilet inside the house either. The famous Irish dry toilet was all we had at the back of the house - it was very primitive.

In the main living area there was a wooden topped table with black painted legs. It was always scrubbed clean and was propped against the panel in the day and dragged out into the middle of the floor for meal times when the few chairs we had dotted around the house were placed around it. We all ate together and for most of the time, we were always served the same meal. Breakfast would be bacon, homemade bread, homemade butter and homemade damson jam with a cup of tea. The evening meal would generally be the same every day and would consist of homegrown vegetables, mainly potatoes, cabbage and carrots and fish or bacon, which my father reared himself in later years. The potatoes were placed on a big plate in the middle of the table and we all had to peel the skins off ourselves. I remember my father always making us eat the fat on the bacon too, "It's good for you," he'd say. There was always plenty of butter for the potatoes and we were never short of the basics such as sugar, tea and salt.

I remember once that the fields behind the house were abundant with mushrooms and we all went out with cans to collect them all. When we got home, my mother got a bed sheet and spread it out on the grass so we could all tip our mushrooms onto it. The mushrooms dried out overnight and the next day she collected them all up and made ketchup. It was the best thing I had ever tasted, it was absolutely delicious. Living such a simple life, I guess she had to be resourceful and she never let us down but my father had a substantial vegetable plot on the other side of the small stretch of canal outside our home which enabled us to live very well. We were never hungry as he grew gooseberries, cabbage, potatoes, carrots, onions and turnips and of course there were the damson trees which always produced huge crops. My father would walk over the top of the lock gates to get to his 'island' plot and he always worked very hard on his planting. I often remember him being out gardening late into the evening and on the back of a full day at work up at The Stackallan Estate.

Our home was situated between Stackallan Bridge, or Broadboyne Bridge as it is sometimes referred to, upstream and Slane Bridge downstream and the riverbank was always and still is a special place to me. Unlike now, the banks of the river were all clean-cut grass with a visible and well-trodden path in the middle where the horses, required for pulling the lighters, once walked. It was an unusual canal in that it was specifically built to help the river traffic navigate the numerous rapids and weirs along the River Boyne but due to the ever-changing conditions of the river it could only be used for part of the year. Five or so locks were on the north bank whilst the rest were on the south bank and when navigating the river, the boatman would walk the horse along the ramparts, pulling the barge behind it on the canal. When travelling upstream, they crossed the river at Englishby's Lock and we would often stand and watch the bargemen manoeuvre the horses on to the top of the lighter, before poling it across the water. They'd get off again at Markey's Lock just next to Stackallan Bridge before continuing their journey along the path on the south side.

Although life for me was one long adventure, for my mother it must have been very different as my father left for work on the Stackallan Estate every morning leaving my mother to spend long days isolated with her growing brood. We had a couple of neighbours but not many. My Aunty Alice, Uncle Edward and numerous cousins lived further downstream beyond Dooner's cottage at Carrickdexter Lock. Our lock and Dooner's Lock were virtually identical. They were built from stone taken from the quarry at the back of our house and the lock gates were painted red. 'Old Dooner' was said to have been a sailor and I think he must have been, as he wasn't always there. I remember he had a huge crucifix tattooed on his chest and it always fascinated me when I saw him working bare chested on his little plot.

Upstream towards Stackallan Bridge, lived the Englishby's. Our two families had been neighbours and known each other some considerable time, my father's baptismal certificate, which I cherish, shows a Tom Englishby was his Godfather back in July 1900. It was quite a little community, helping each other when necessary and in reality I didn't come into contact with many more people other than that for several years. Occasionally there would be the excitement of a hunt from Beauparc House, riding through on the opposite side of the river and we would all stop to watch the excitement, my mother included. They would ride off as quickly as they came and Mum would go back into the house to carry on with her jobs while we carried on watching and waving wildly until the last one disappeared from view, before picking up with whatever game we were playing. I remember that the riders would all be dressed up in

29

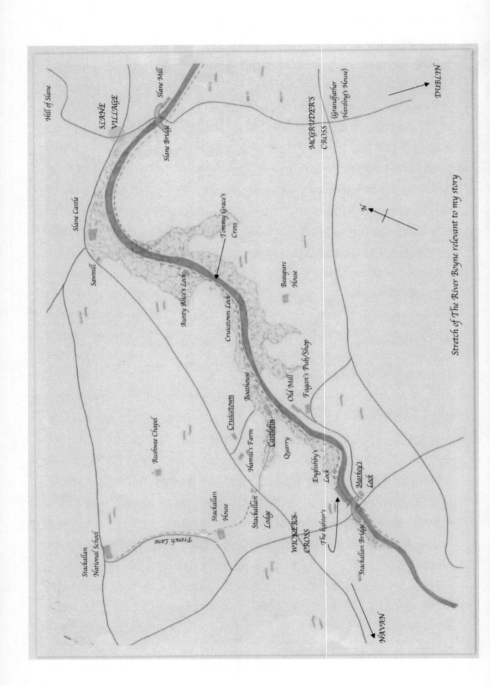

Stretch of The River Boyne relevant to my story

red jackets, they would jump the gate into the field on the opposite bank and there was lots of noise and merriment as they passed by. It was always quite a thrill to witness the commotion of a passing hunt. The Lambert's lived up at Beauparc House and although I never met Lord Lambert, I did meet his wife and his son in later years. They would regularly call up to my father's office at Stackallan House to pay for the grazing land they rented for their cattle and I recall that Lady Lambert was always dressed up to the nines in a fur coat and jewels!

My mother would work hard around the house all day every day leaving the confines of the cottage only on a Saturday afternoon. She would leave us in our father's charge, take her bike in all weathers and cycle the five or six miles to Navan for groceries. How she must have loved that time on her own - her own little bit of freedom.

Visitors to Castlefin were few and far between but Cissy Dooner who was the daughter of our nearest neighbour regularly passed by. Cissy who was a teenager when I was a little boy, would often walk past our house on her way to the small shop on the opposite side of the river. She would always stop and ask my mother if she needed anything and on her way back she would come in for a cup of tea and the two of them could chat for hours some days. Thinking back, apart from the people my mother met in Navan on a Saturday, Cissy Dooner was really the only person outside of the family that I saw her speak to on a regular basis.

The canal lock was only about six or seven yards from the front door and therefore to keep us safe and reduce my mother's worry when we were tiny, my father built a wooden slatted fence around the house which 'penned us in'. It was nailed to the side walls of the house and surrounded a grassy area at the front of the house which was divided by a simple path that led from the gate up to the front door. We could see through the slats but could not go

31

beyond to where it was dangerous as the little gate was always bolted, again from outside and out of reach from little hands. I vividly remember watching the last lighter going down the canal and the three men working on the boat were the first people I remember seeing, other than my immediate family and usual neighbours. I was playing in the pen with my sisters and we stopped to watch the excitement, I must have only been about three or four at the time. Visitors were rare but to watch them running around and operate the lock and to watch the lighter lift up in the lock was mesmerising. I remember my mother being equally excited and she boiled water and filled the kettle to make them all a pot of tea. They had their own mugs on the boat and when their job was done and they returned the teapot, they brought a banana for each of us. It was around 1931 and it was the first time I had ever seen a banana.

I hardly ever remember seeing any of my relations whilst we lived down at Castlefin other than my Uncle Tom (Reilly) who would row over to see us from Beauparc or my Uncle Peter (Harding) who came down once or twice to say hello. The first time I met Peter, I remember being very small and I remember that he brought a pencil and a book that was full of plain paper with him. He sat me down beside him and drew me a donkey. I was absolutely mesmerised. Isn't it strange that the simplest things make such lastings impressions, but I had never seen anyone draw like that before and create pictures on the page - I thought what he did was magical!

Other visitors included two old men who lived in the lane at the back of the house. We called one, Monk Mooney. He wore big baggy pants and had a huge white beard and I never knew his real name at the time although I've since found out it was Joseph. He was always chopping wood and stacking it up outside his house. The other chap was called Barney McKeever and neither of them did any work so I don't know how they lived, from hand to mouth I expect. I think they may have been related, they lived together with other family members in a small cottage that my nephew lives in now, in the lane that leads down to the old quarry. Dick Brady, his brothers and sister Maggie lived next door to them.

Barney McKeever was a very keen fisherman and he would often come down and fish the River Boyne from the banks by our home. One day he said, "Come with me John," and he took me along the riverbank until we came to a place suitable for hand fishing. "You look one way while I look the other," he said. Of course I was meant to warn him if Willie Kerrigan, the water bailiff, came by while he was poaching for fish. Willie worked for the Slane Castle estate and lived up at Carrickdexter. So Barney took his jacket off and rolled his sleeve up to his elbow, he lay down on the bank so as not to cast a shadow over the water and he gently put his hand in the water and started to tickle the trout. I was so engrossed by what he was doing that I failed to provide the appropriate warning when Willie Kerrigan, who rode up and down the riverbank on his bike looking for poachers, stumbled upon us. All of a sudden we heard, "Now Barney, let it go." I don't know who jumped more, me, Barney or the fish! All I could think of that night while I lay there trying to catch my sleep was the silly song I had made up about him:-

Barney McKeever went fishing,
It was on a nice summer's day,
He carried a rod,
and this is no cod,
he'd frighten the salmon away...

Barney was also remembered fondly by many for walking his little donkey, which we called 'Barney's Ass'. He generally used the donkey to pull his cart and they would often be seen trundling along the lanes pulling logs, hay or produce that he had grown in the field. We would often see others fishing along the river bank and of course most had the required permits to fish, unlike Barney. There was a chap who worked up at Slane Castle that we called 'Banks Brennan' because he was always on the riverbank fishing and he was well known to us all. He famously caught a salmon that weighed in at 39lbs and it was the talk of the place for days as it took him three hours to reel it in. The River Boyne was not just a beautiful river, it was also a bountiful river.

During the winter time when the heavy rains came, the river levels would rise considerably and these frequent floods would render the canals redundant. The wind would howl like hell in the trees and when the water raced over the top of the lock gates it would make terrifying gushing noises. The groans from the trees and roars from the fast flowing waters would echo long and deep into the night and the wind and rain would often wake us in the early hours. It was dreadfully dark at night, there were no lights and no-one lived nearby, we were really quite isolated and I was often afraid at night as a small boy. I often wonder if this is why I always had a light on in the house at night, even when I was an old man, I never liked to sleep in the dark! I remember hearing a story about my Uncle Christy who lived down at Castlefin as a young man. Back then, the Black and Tans were prevalent in the area and one evening, keen to speak to Christie, they hid themselves in woods around the house, hoping to surprise him and question him. Foolishly whilst tucked up in their hiding places, they lit up cigarettes which glowed in the dark as they puffed away and this subsequently alerted my grandmother who was sitting in front of the fire inside the cottage to their presence. She watched them through the cottage window which overlooked the woods and with a little quick thinking, she calmly sent my father out to find and warn Christy not to come home that evening. As a consequence

Christy was able to keep a low profile until their interest in him petered out. I was always amused that such a simple mistake foiled their plan but it was one of the advantages of being so remote, or at least I like to think Christy thought so!

The heavy rains always brought concern to my parents, the house was very basic and very old and I often recall us all huddling in front of the fire to keep warm and dry. On one occasion after some heavy rains, my mother asked me to collect some water from the stream that ran directly under the house so that she could wash the potatoes. The rain had subsided and it was dry enough for me to venture outside but the water level had risen considerably and the steps at the side of the house which we used to reach the water's edge were beginning to get covered in water. As I stepped down, the water immediately came up to my knees and as I lowered the bucket into the swollen stream, the force of the water dragged the bucket and me with it, directly under the house. My sister Betty happened to be watching from the window above and screamed when she saw me fall, which immediately alerted my mother to my peril. She reacted so quickly, dropped everything, ran outside and jumped fully clothed straight into the water further downstream. After bumping and banging my way under the house, I was relieved to see my mother standing in the stream waiting for me when I came through the other side. She snatched me up coughing and spluttering and saved me from being dragged off to the fast flowing River Boyne, where I would have probably perished. She took me inside, took off my wet clothes, wrapped me in a blanket and sat me in front of the fire to dry off. Everyone was traumatised by those events, particularly my mother as she never told my father what happened that day. Clearly, life down on the riverbank was getting increasingly more difficult.

However, in the summer of 1931, after unusual heavy rains, flash foods caused havoc throughout the whole area and it was later reported that both the River Boyne and the River Blackwater in Navan, flooded their banks. It started off as any other evening for us but living on the water's edge we couldn't help but notice that the water was unusually high that night although we had no idea about the drama that would soon unfold. After the usual bedtime routine we were all tucked in and fast asleep when we were all of a sudden woken by my mother who was shrieking "Dick, Dick, the house is shaking". Dad came flying out of his bedroom half-dressed, opened up the front door and soon realised the urgency. Dressed only in our nightclothes, he ushered us all up the steep riverbank at the back of the house to his garden shed where we huddled together to escape from the rising water. I remember that my mother ran with one of the smaller children wrapped in blankets in her arms as they were far too little to fend for themselves and that my dad then collected all the bed linen and everything he could lay his hands on to make us more comfortable.

The force of the water running underneath the house had caused the whole house to shake and on leaving the front door we could just make out the water flooding over the top of the ramparts. We tried as best as possible to get comfortable in that shed but all we had to sleep on were boxes and benches. In fact, I don't remember my parents being in the shed with us at all that night and to this day, I can still smell the wood of the shed and smell the earth from my father's tools. None of us got much sleep that night, if any at all, it was a frightening experience and even at such a young age, I recognised the danger of the rising waters. As the eldest of the children huddled together in that shed, I tried my best to calm my brothers and sisters but we were all anxious especially once we were left on our own. I now wonder if the reason why my parents weren't there was because they were forced to work through the night to save the belongings from the house while we were left to sleep in a safer and more secure environment.

The plan was to wait for the water to subside before venturing out again but unbeknown to us, my Uncle Jack who was walking across Slane Bridge the next morning, noticed the excessive swell in the river and knew that we would be in trouble. He sent Christy Cassidy, a local taxi driver through the town to rescue us and this is when I experienced my very first car ride.

Uncle John 'Jack' Reilly

Christy left his car at the top of the lane that ran passed the quarry at the back of the house and made his way down through the woods until he found us. It was such a relief for my mother who later told me that that night was the most frightened that she had ever been. Not only did we have to deal with the rising waters, but it was cold, pitch black and the noise from the raging river was deafening. To a small boy, it was yet another adventure but to my parents, who saw the reality, it must have been a dreadful experience.

Within a short period of time, my fear had turned into excitement and I remember stepping up into Christy's car. He had instructions to take us all back to my Uncle Jack's house and as we drove there I remember looking out of the car window, and my first thought was that the hedges were moving. It didn't take long for me to work out what was happening and my parents both laughed when it dawned on me that it was the motion from the moving car that made it look like the hedges were moving! I was completely absorbed in the journey and of course I was seeing places I had never seen before - a whole new world had opened up to me. I distinctly remember the smell of the leather upholstery in that car and being overjoyed when we were allowed to stay at my Uncle Jack and Aunty Mary's in Fennor until the waters subsided. Their house was the only house in the area which had an upstairs so that made the adventure even better as this was something else that was new to me. This was the beginning of a great relationship I shared with my Uncle Jack who sadly never had any children of his own.

He took an immediate shine to me and he would sit me on his knees and let me play with his fob watch, which was given to me, many years later by my Aunty Mary. It has been one of my most treasured possessions but it is now in the safe hands of my own son Damian, who will hopefully pass it onto my grandson Edward, for safekeeping in the future.

The watch was a gift to Uncle Jack by The London Metropolitan Police, in recognition of long service to them. He had moved to London as a young man looking for work and spent many years there before retiring home to Ireland. As he never had any children of his own I presume the reason I was gifted his watch was because I was his godson. The details included in the engraving on the back of the watch enabled my daughter Amanda to trace his career in the Metropolitan police as well as a copy of his application form which provided a thorough description of him and of course, addresses he lived at while he was in London. This was the very first task on the quest for information about the REILLY family history and I was in awe that so much information was readily available. What a journey it set us off on.

Whilst trying to attach a time frame to my memory of the floods, my daughter Amanda uncovered a newspaper article that reported the impact of those events in June 1931 to a family in Navan. She read the story aloud to me and I was instantly transported back to the cold, wet and dark of that very long night. "I wonder why they didn't publish my story," I said, but of course being so remote, no-one would have really known anything about us and the situation we found ourselves in. Without telling me, Amanda then contacted a local Irish newspaper to see if they would be interested in a human interest story - my story. She explained my circumstances and the fact that we had delved into their archives to research further and as a consequence and to my immense delight The Meath Chronicle published my story in 2015, 84 year later. I was tickled pink, there was I, a lad from the riverside on a full page spread in The Meath Chronicle. This naturally brought all sorts of phone calls from my family at home when they read all about it - how I enjoyed my little moment in the spotlight, I felt quite the celebrity. I don't suppose there will be many around now that recall the events of that evening but to me it is a lasting if not terrifying memory.

The following year, 1932, was another memorable year for me because this was the year I saw my first aeroplane, something that we now take for granted and think of as nothing special, but to a boy with no access to books or television, this was quite a spectacle. I was out walking with my father on the river bank and we were strolling along chatting and looking at the swans, the water hens and the ducks, I can't even remember where we were going. All of a sudden there was a loud noise in the sky and I remember that we were both startled. My father explained that what we'd just seen was called an aeroplane and because it had flown so low over the river and treetops, I could see so much of its detail. I could see the small wheels underneath the carriage, the propeller and the wings which had shiny silver spokes in between them. The sun glinted off the chrome as it flew past and we shielded our eyes as we followed the plane travel through the sky. To add to my excitement two more planes flew over some moments later, I had never seen anything like it before and I couldn't wait to get back home to tell everyone about the spectacle that I had seen. I later learned that they were there for the celebrations up on The Hill of Slane, linked to the Eucharistic Congress In Dublin, that's how I came to know that it was specifically 1932 when I saw them. I would have been five.

Overall, I don't recall spending huge amounts of time with my father, he was not one for conversation and for most of the time he would be out of the house working. Every evening though, he'd sit me on his knee and I was allowed to play with the watch and chain that he would take out of his waistcoat pocket. He was a tall man, he had black, greying hair that he brushed back off his face and he always wore a navy blue suit and a white shirt and tie. I never saw him in a sports coat, or casual attire, he was always very smart but I guess that came from having a job of some importance up at Stackallan Estate. I don't know when he became a cattleman or when he started working up at Stackallan House but I do remember seeing a photograph of him in his shirt sleeves, as a younger man working with others as they transported timber on a lorry. He didn't share many family stories or much about himself and with me moving away from home in 1949 the opportunities to discuss things together passed us by.

Like myself, I don't think he had much schooling and I know for sure that it was my mother that did most of the household correspondence so I suspect he went straight into farming from school, like most young men that grew up in Ireland at that time. I wish more than anything that he had shared more family stories with me, I wish I had asked more questions when I was older - how easily family history is lost for the sake of time spent together.

When I was five years old, I also did my first grown up errand for my mother. She asked me to go and collect some groceries from the local shop, which was on the opposite south bank of the river by the old cotton mill; a derelict and run-down building in the latter years of my time living there, in fact a derelict and run down building still.

It was used as a sawmill at one point and I remember seeing the water wheel go around very slowly but I don't think the sawmill venture was particularly successful as it didn't last very long. It was a considerable walk for a little boy and I had to cross over Stackallan Bridge to Fagan's Pub, which true to Irish tradition, doubled up as a shop as well. Fagan's was a big stone building with six large windows but it was very overgrown with ivy back then, unlike today. It's a beautiful spot and I always pull up the car there when I visit home. There's nothing much to see but for me I can see myself playing as a young boy on the opposite bank and my mind fills with so many happy memories. I love to stand and listen to the rushing water even today, in fact I'd have to say it's one of my all-time favourite places, especially in the Autumn.

Back then, it was where we bought sugar, tea and other basic supplies but of course we had to pass through the 'pub' which was its primary purpose, if we needed anything. It was frequented by the farmhands who would walk home along the riverbank at night after their long day in the fields and it was the shop that Cissy Dooner would visit when she passed by our house. This time however, it was my turn to go all by myself. I remember my mother giving me clear instructions of the route to take and I clutched a list that she had carefully written out. I know this because although I couldn't read properly, I recognised the word 'sugar' on the piece of paper but other than that, I don't know what else I was sent to collect. I didn't know what to expect on my journey either and there was an element of uncertainty as well as excitement as I set off and when I think about it now, I think my mother took a chance asking me to go all that way on my own. Was she late on in pregnancy with another child and perhaps didn't want to risk going herself? Had Cissy not called as usual and were we so short of basic supplies that she took the risk of sending me, while she stayed at home with the younger children? Or did she just think I was ready to go on my own?

It was an approximate five-mile round trip which was a long way for little legs and it was an adventure that took me all afternoon and one that I never forgot. It took me upstream along the footpath on the north bank of the river, past Englishby's, across Stackallan Bridge and an immediate left turn onto the road running along the south bank. I passed a couple of cottages, although at the time I had no idea who lived there. I felt like I had walked into a whole new world and I explored slowly, but above anything else, the thing I remember most was the silence. It was incredibly peaceful on that walk and I often think back to those innocent days with great fondness.

I learnt to swim up at Stackallan Bridge years later with a lad called Tommy Finnegan from Wicker's Cross and a lad called Matty Wall who was a dead keen swimmer. Tommy watched me swim from one side of the river to the other at that spot, keeping a close eye on me during my first attempt and he even tried to teach me how to dive. There was a spot close by where the water was really deep, it was called the lugaree and we'd dive off the three lighters that seemed to be permanently tied up there. I made such a hash of my first attempt and came up spluttering and gasping for breath, I never did it again. I'm proud that I at least tried though. We spent many happy times there, fishing, swimming and just generally larking about as young lads do. I can see all their faces as clear as anything - great days and great memories.

Even in my early twenties, and after we had moved house, I would take myself off after Mass and walk down to Slane Bridge, along the ramparts and up through the fields at Carrickdexter, before heading home along the main Slane to Navan Road. It was a good long walk but I loved the solitude and most times, I wouldn't

View of the north bank of the River Boyne, taken from the old saw mill and the house that was once Fagan's Pub.

pass a single soul. I recognised all the bird song, I knew the name of all types of trees and it was easy for me to recognise any changes to the area despite the passage of time. There was never any river traffic as such, only small boats that were used by familiar faces to cross from one side of the River Boyne to the other. When I was small and lived at the riverbank, Dick Brady, who lived in one of the cottages in the lane above would walk down to our house every morning through the woods, along the ramparts and use the boat that was stored in our boat house to row across to Beauparc on the other side. He worked on the farm that belonged to Lord Lambert at Beauparc House and this shortcut saved him a lot of time and effort. Walking around was not the preferred option for him or for many others. My Uncle Tom who also worked at Beauparc and lived on the south bank of the river would occasionally use the boat to come and visit us.

I watched my father use this same boat to go bobbing for eels on many occasions. One particular time, not long after we had had a flood, I remember him rowing the boat into the middle of the River Boyne with a friend whilst I stayed firmly on the riverbank. They knew that there would be an abundance of eels after the floodwaters and they were keen to harvest them as soon as

43

possible. In preparation, he dug the garden and collected a bucketful of worms which he laced together on a long piece of string. Bringing the string back through them he created a cluster of worms the size of a small football. He then tied this to the end of a short rod which he specifically kept for this purpose and when out in the middle of the river he would stand up in the boat and dip the bait in the water to attract them. When he lifted the rod and line, I remember being surprised at the number of eels hanging there - his line was full of eels squirming and wriggling. He shook them off into a large tub that he placed in the middle of the boat and when he brought the catch in, the tub was almost full and there were many more wriggling around on the bottom of the boat. The catch was so heavy that my father and his friend each had to hold a handle of the tub to carry it to the house. The eels didn't crawl out or try to escape but he quickly covered them with salt to kill them. Once word spread about the extent of the catch, people were coming for days to collect eels from us and, as it was a community for giving and sharing, my father did not charge anyone, he simply gave away what he could not use himself.

I watched both my parents catch and prepare eels many times so much so that in 2009, I took great delight in showing my daughter and granddaughter how to do the very same. I had asked my local fishmonger 'Scully' to bring me four eels and to everyone's surprise they arrived in a bucket, very much alive. Even Scully was quite shocked, a young man who up until this point had only ever dealt with dead fish. Heaven help us, what a commotion I caused when I appeared at my daughter's one day with two of these live eels in a bucket. I asked for the drum of salt which I duly sprinkled over them and said I would return the next day. My granddaughter Jennifer, who was about 14 at the time, gave me lectures on animal cruelty but to me it was just survival, it was what I did and how we lived back then, why should it be any different now? I returned the next day and of course the eels were dead so I sliced though the eel's skin behind its ears and pinned it to the garden fence through it's head.

2008 - Preparing the eel supper

Taking a strong pair of pliers I then proceeded to skin the eels before gutting them. Watched and photographed because it was such a strange occurrence to those more used to this part of the food process being done for them, I then went on to tell Amanda how to cook them and simply suggested slicing them into three-inch lengths and frying them in butter and rosemary, just like my mother always did. "Grandpa, that's gross," my granddaughter Jennifer exclaimed, "I'm not going to eat any of that, that's disgusting!" With great enthusiasm Amanda set to and once the delicious smell started permeating through the house, who was first in the queue? You guessed it - Jennifer!! To everyone's surprise, the eel supper went down a treat, I was as pleased as punch, as pleased as I was the night my father went bobbing for eels on the River Boyne and brought home that enormous catch.

My father was not a frequent fisherman but he did set off with rod and line once in a while and it was watching him catch all those eels that sparked my own interest in fishing. Being only five or six years old I was only allowed to fish in the canal where I could see all the eels at the bottom. I would attach a worm to the line and I knew I had a catch when the cork I put on the end bobbed under the water. The first eel I ever caught was only small and I was very excited, although quite unsure what to do with it once I pulled it in. I remember putting it down on the riverbank while I put more bait on for a second cast and while I was preoccupied with this task, the little blighter escaped back into the water. I learned the hard way and never made that mistake again but was always disappointed that I couldn't show Mammy that I had caught my first fish.

It must also have been around 1932 that my mother asked me to take her 'clucking hen' over to Mrs. Dooner, as her own hen refused to sit on its own eggs in the nest. Cissy had stopped by to ask my mother if they could borrow one of our hens and even though I thought this was funny, I wasn't very amused when I realised that it was I that had to get involved in this particular chore. I didn't like the hens much and although they roamed freely around the house and garden and provided us with fresh eggs daily, I had also witnessed my mother killing the hens on occasion for our dinner and had not enjoyed watching that. My mother would hold a hen by the legs and neck and stretch it until it went limp and then she would get a hatchet and chop its head off. They were called Sussex hens and I often watched as she removed all the white feathers, cleaned it out and put it in the pot to boil over the fire. This was just the routine way of life for us then and of course I didn't object to eating the freshly cooked chicken when it was placed on the table or any of the eggs the hens produced which my mother would boil and serve up with bread and butter for dipping. I most certainly didn't object when Mammy served the delicious soup the next day, made from the chicken leftovers, mixed with vegetables and parsley from the garden. So regardless of my dislike of being up close and personal to the hens my mother insisted that I carry this particular broody hen to Mrs. Dooner to help her eggs hatch and even though I must have only been five years old at the time, I set off unattended once more for the short familiar half mile journey downstream. For some reason my mother made me put on a white fur coat. Was it to soothe the bird? I had to fold my arms around the hen and carry it tightly in front of me, holding on to its feet and legs. I was only half way there when the hen, who must have been pretty frightened itself, shit all over both me and the white fur coat. The shock from this, coupled with the smell which was awful, forced me to let go of the hen and it flew off into the woods. Even more upset now because I had lost the hen, I went home crying to my mother and all she did was laugh. Whether the hen ever returned home or ended up with Mrs. Dooner I never knew.

My dislike for the hens and their mess went one step further when some months later, my mum asked me to go to the hen shed and collect the eggs for breakfast. I diligently collected all the eggs that I could carry and placed them carefully into the small basket so that they wouldn't break. I thought I was doing a good job but my mother wasn't best pleased when I didn't bring back as many as usual. "Is this all there is John?", she asked, to which I replied, "Well, there was a few with poo on but I threw them away". She was so cross with me that day and I got a real scolding for throwing away good food. Her anger mellowed with time and I remember her telling that story years later, "Oh John doesn't eat eggs with poo on" and she laughed heartily.

My mother Kitty Reilly on wash day c1935

I often think how hard life must have been for my mother and tasks we regard as simple and take for granted nowadays must have been dreadfully difficult for her. I remember her washing the bedclothes and how diligently she worked. This task generally took most of her morning and she would begin by setting up a wooden wash tub up on two chairs or a small table outside the front of the house. She would collect water from the small stream that ran under the house and boil this little by little in the huge kettle over the open fire, filling the wash tub until there was enough water for the job in hand. After scrubbing and scrubbing the sheets, she would lay them out on flat, freshly mown grassy patches at the back of the house weighing them down with clean, round, smooth stones that she kept specifically for this job. The sun would shine down on them and they would be dry in no time. Everything smelled clean and fresh and I can still see her now, beavering away. How she managed this task in the winter, I'll never know! I seem to remember that she also had a small clothes lines for the baby clothes as I often recall the clothes blowing in the wind at the side of the house.

Meal times were very different too as there was no such thing as convenience foods for us. My father would often bring home freshly caught fish or rabbit to make a change from the usual bacon. The rabbit would have to be skinned and cleaned and once, I remember my mother taking a rabbit down to the stream to wash away the blood and finish getting it ready for the pan. As she was busy washing the rabbit, two huge eels came up and started nibbling it and being as resourceful as ever, she quickly sliced off a piece of the rabbit, tied it to a line and fishing rod and allowed the eels to feast. With one swift tug, we now had two huge eels for dinner as well as the prepared rabbit. Now it was our turn to feast. On another occasion, I remember my father brought home a huge pike that he had caught. He was more than satisfied with his catch as it was as big as any salmon that we had had and he proudly lay it on the table for my mother to prepare. On taking a knife to it to cut it open and clean it out, it caused quite a commotion when it started flapping around on the table. One more quick thud from Mammy and it soon lay flat and still again!!

49

My mother always kept the cottage neat and tidy, prettied up with clean net curtains over the two small windows, and occasionally fresh cut flowers from her garden were placed on the table. The house was bedecked with a handful of pots, bowls and utensils but worthy of special note were the large Holy pictures which would be decorated with holly, ivy and flowers from the woods at Christmas time or on Holy Days of Obligation. To this day, I still have my mother's old irons that she used for pressing the clothes and I guess they would be considered antiques now. They required the use of a hot brick which was warmed up on the fire and placed into a compartment at the back. As it cooled it was replaced with a second hot brick and this process continued until the ironing was complete. It was far removed from

Kitty Reilly lacemaking in 1943

simply flicking a switch to turn the iron on as we do today. Most of what we had was practical, there was little by way of decoration but I do remember the family clock and the mirror that hung on the wall. I would watch my father shave himself in that mirror every morning and even though it was placed too high up for me to see myself in, my father did often lift me so I could have a look at myself.

In reality, my mother spent all of her time washing, cleaning, shopping, baking, cooking and mending. Her hands were always busy and even when sitting chatting with Cissy Dooner, or my father in the evening, the knitting bag or sewing basket would come out. As well as being skilled at lace making, she taught us all to knit, me included and after our tea we would all huddle around the fire with our knitting and talk about our day. I'm sure my grandson Edward who knows only football and computers would find that quite amusing.

I never saw any books in the house, in fact none of us could read very well until we went to school and for me that wasn't until September 1935, when I was seven, almost eight years old. During these early years we didn't even have a radio, but my father, who never went to the pub in the evening when we were young, would read the daily paper, often reading articles out loud that he thought were of interest to my mother. I don't think my father had much by way of schooling, I'm not sure my mother did either but regardless it was my mother that dealt with all the correspondence in our house, presumably because my father was out at work most of the time. Every moment was precious and I never remember seeing my mother idle. She made all our clothes, mainly dresses for the girls although she did make a shirt for me once. She bought my trousers but I only ever remember having one pair at a time. I called them 'ma breeches' and they were long navy-blue shorts. I never remember wearing underpants, but I do remember my mother making underclothes for the girls and I can see her now, threading elastic through garments with a very long needle. She knit my socks too which came up to my knees but as a young boy, my knees were always bare and full of scratches. I also had my own boots with laces, a must for scrambling and foraging in the woods.

My mother would also make her own damson jam using the damsons from our own trees on the little island garden on the other side of the canal, she would make her own soda bread using the buttermilk from the goats we kept and there was of course many other delicious treats. When she baked bread or cakes, I can see her now placing the dough into the huge black iron pot and then hanging it up on the chains over the open fire. With the lid firmly in place on the pot, she would scoop up the hot embers from the fire, which she called 'gree-sha' and placed some on the top to help the bread cook from both ends. Her soda bread was extra special and when Amanda makes soda bread for me at home, the smell and taste transports me back to those bygone days in an instant. Just like Mammy, Amanda would cut thick slices, griddle then on both sides and smother them with homemade jam … Mmmmmm … My mother made so much jam there was always enough for everyone and anyone that did visit generally walked away with a full pot. I can still see old Johnny Hamill sitting at our table eating it directly from the jar with a spoon and he never failed to take home what was left in the jar she served up to him. The Hamills were farmers and were very good to my family. They had cows on land at the back of the woods and they would visit every time they came to check on them. In-between ours and Dooner's Lock, although closer to Dooner's than ours, there was part of a ruined bridge at the river's edge where farmers used to come and dip their sheep before they were sheared. I used to love it when 'Old Hamill' brought his sheep down, "I'm here to bath the sheep, John. Are you coming to help?" With my mother's permission, I would walk along the ramparts with Johnny to the 'sheep dip' and watched as he tied a rope around the neck of the sheep before throwing them into the river one at a time. I'd do my best to join in with the task but in reality, I think I was probably more of a hindrance than a help. It was great fun and I felt important to be involved although I always ended up getting completely drenched as I generally pranced around in the water with each of the sheep. Occasionally the Hamill's would bring us sacks of potatoes or vegetables from their farm if we were running short and when I was older I occupied myself by doing odd jobs on their farm. When my father started to keep his own cattle, the Hamills let him graze them on their land.

Jimmy Hamill, my brother Patsy and my father c1945

Every day we would wake up to my mother cooking the breakfast. She would always cook bacon and it was a great smell first thing in the morning. Bacon was the only meat we ate really at that time, although we did enjoy chicken occasionally and especially at Christmas. It was such a simple life. Before eating, my mother would place a basin of hot water on the table and wash our faces, hands and knees with a flannel and soap, we were then allowed to tuck in. Bath times were much more exciting and eventful as we had a big round bath which was zinc and therefore orange on the outside although on the inside I seem to remember that it was like ice blue. It was hung up outside in a shed and she did struggle every time she had to bring it into the house but every so often she'd fill it up with boiling water from the kettle and top this up with cold water from the brook. We shared a bath and I remember three of us being in the bath together many times. I was always first out and I remember sitting on her knee while she dried me off. On one occasion I jumped back in as I was having too much of a good time but she smacked me over the head and shouted at me to get out! I thought it was funny but she obviously didn't. We never used a toothbrush and despite this poor start in oral hygiene, at 89, I still have my own teeth. Not many of them but they are at least my own!

3

Cruicetown

My sister Maureen was born in 1933 so I suspect the growing family, along with the fear of living in an area prone to flooding, forced the decision to move out of the Boyne Valley. As far as I know, I think we were the first to move out of that riverside community, as the Dooner's left to live on the Navan Road 18 months later. Whether the Englishbys moved on before us I'm not sure as I only saw them once or twice as a boy when I passed by their house on the way to the shop. My parents would have known but as a boy I didn't pay too much attention to that sort of thing. So out of the blue one sunny July morning in 1935, when I was seven and a half years old, I was told to gather up some of our belongings as we were going to live in a new house. As well as it being a time of excitement, it was also a time of sadness for me to be leaving the banks of The Boyne and the lock keeper's cottage, the cottage that had served the Reilly family for quite some time, but we were moving to higher ground where it was safer and I understood the need for that too. We didn't move very far, just a short distance up to the lane at the back of the house which as far as I know was never named. Our address was simply Cruicetown and that's the way it still is.

There was no great planning or talk about the new house as far as I was aware although my father did take me on a walk a few times up that way and I remember seeing the footings of the new place all laid out between wooden batons and string. At the time, I didn't realise what I was looking at but I do remember being intrigued by it all and wondered how a house would ever get there. It was built by the Council at a time of development for the area but my father signed a contract to purchase and paid 1s/3d per week for the rest of his life. My younger brother Seamus told me that when my mother died in 1993, there was still a small debt outstanding that the Council insisted was paid off and at the original agreed rate! During that first visit with my father I remember him being concerned that the side wall of the house was too near to the lane and after circling the footprint of the house many times, he set to and spent some considerable time adjusting the layout to a position and size that he preferred. He was indeed a 'Wiley' Reilly!

Amanda, Martin and Rita at the house at Cruicetown c1963

I think my parents must have borrowed a horse and cart to carry the bigger items from the edge of the woods up to the new place, maybe we even made use of Barney's ass but my specific task was to carry my mother's precious paraffin lamp and I did so very, very carefully. "Don't you break the globe or spill that paraffin on your clothes," Mammy exclaimed, so I took extra care with every step I took. I walked through the woods, with my brothers and sisters, carrying what I could and apart from the lamp and globe, I remember taking a chair and a few other small items on separate journeys. On reaching the new house, the first thing my father did was take the lamp off me and hang it up on the wall where it was safe.

This house was much bigger than the one we had left behind and instead of us all sharing just one room, we now had the luxury of having a large kitchen, THREE bedrooms, a small scullery AND an outside toilet. It was designed to my mother's liking and all that day she was like the cat that got the cream. As the furniture was put in to place I remember running around with my brother and sisters in the huge field at the back of the house. In fact, the house was totally surrounded by grass at that time apart from a small gravel path that led up to the front door. I remember there being a lot of excitement and us having a lot of fun that day as we all familiarised ourselves with our new surroundings.

As before, the house was built of stone, covered in rendering and this time painted cream whilst the sills and front door were painted in the familiar green, everything was clean and fresh. As before we had a slate roof and one chimney, although this time we had two fireplaces, one in the kitchen where my mother did all the cooking and the other in the bedroom allocated to my sisters. The rooms were all of a good size, the biggest of which was the combined kitchen and living area, which was in the centre of the house and this was the size of the whole house that we had left behind. Every window in the house had brand new lace curtains and the bedrooms had scatter mats here and there. The main room in the house however had new red floor tiles and remained uncovered. It seemed like we had moved into a Palace.

The settle bed was brought in and placed directly under the window on the far side of the kitchen. It continued to act as a seat in the day and a bed at night so as a consequence, my brother Liam and I slept in the kitchen until such time as we got a bed and moved into what eventually became our bedroom. My sisters however, who were six, five and two years old by this time, had the luxury of new beds in the bedroom beside the scullery. The scrubbed wooden table was placed against the kitchen wall between the two remaining bedroom doors, the clock was hung on the wall above it and not far from that was the mirror that my father continued to shave in every morning. As before, at meal times the table was dragged into the middle of the room so that we could all sit around and as before we all kept the same places we used to sit in. My mother sat with her back to the field and faced the front garden, whilst my father sat with his back to the lane, facing the open fire. Old habits die hard! There was still no mains electricity, gas or water and my mother continued to cook on an open fire, which she surrounded with her cast iron griddles, pots, pans and irons that were the basics of all traditional Irish kitchens. The black cast iron kitchen range, which occupied pride of place in later years, wasn't fitted until long after I left home in 1949.

Moving to the new house also meant that we had new neighbours and we now lived on the same lane as Barney McKeever, Monk Mooney and Dick Brady. Around the corner on the main Slane to Navan Road was the entrance to old Johnnie Hamill's farm. Other than that I didn't really know anybody else, although it wasn't long before we became firm friends with Paddy Doggert, The Feelys, The Meades and Biddie Brien and her family. These all lived not too far away and they all became regular visitors to our house over the years.

Mrs. Brien was one of the first to welcome us to the new house and she and my mother soon became great friends spending a lot of time in each others houses. They became considerable figureheads in the locality and were 'handy-women', the term given to the ladies called out to tend to births and deaths in the community. When somebody died, it was their job to prepare the dead for the wake, a common Irish ritual when everyone came to the bedside to say the rosary and celebrate the life of the deceased. It was their responsibility to tidy the house of the deceased, wash the body down, make the bed nice for the dead and finally lay the body out with a crucifix and with rosary beads, which were placed neatly in their fingers. They would light candlesticks and sit beside the body, greeting visitors to the house as they came to pay their respects. I remember my mother telling me about the time they attended to Maggie Brady, Dick Brady's sister, who lived further down the lane from us. Maggie was always a little unkempt and the hems on her skirts were always higgledy-piggledy. Her underskirts would always hang below her dress and if any of my sisters or friends ever turned out like this by accident, it was quite commonplace to ridicule them by saying "Ah, look at you, you have a look of Maggie Brady about you!" Invariably this did not go down well with those that knew her and when I'd say it to my wife and daughter many, many years later, they hadn't a clue what I was talking about. They had never heard of her of course! When my mother and Biddie actually went to do their duty and prepare Maggie's body, they were astounded to find out when washing her hair that she had been dying it with boot polish and her thick black hair was in fact as white as snow!

When it came to helping out at births, they simply supported those due to deliver their baby using their own experiences of pregnancy and labour along with information they had learned from older women. As a young boy, I can remember my mother being called out late at night on numerous occasions and always without any grumbling or fuss, she would simply collect her things and head off with Biddie into the night.

4

Stackallan National School

With the new house came new routines for us all, new chores and new responsibilities. For me, this included school. Whilst living at the lock house, I didn't know anything about school, my parents had never spoken of it and of course I didn't really come into contact with any other children who went to any, we just lived too far away from the nearest one and I was too little to go so far on my own so I simply stayed at home. Thinking back, maybe getting their children an education was a priority for my parents and this was another reason why we moved house. They could both read and write so they would have gone to school themselves, although I am not really sure where.

We had only been in the new house a few weeks when Paddy Doggert, one of our new neighbours, came to accompany me to my new school. It was early September 1934, I was seven years old as I distinctly remember having my eighth birthday in school, my first away from home. I imagine my own father would have left early to go to work, if it was a Monday, he would have had to set off for the Navan Market seven miles away and the agricultural fair that took place there every week. So I guess Paddy was asked to take me so I didn't get lost and this would have also allowed my mother to stay at home with my brothers and sisters.

I don't know why I didn't go to Slane School, instead I went to Stackallan National School which was about two and half miles away from our new house and of course the journey was always made on foot. In the summer months we would often go in our bare feet too, such happy carefree days. We'd all do it and we couldn't wait to discard our boots and socks and I remember on April 1st one year, my friend Liam Feely and I took our boots and socks off on our

Stackallan National School House

Three Generations: John Reilly, Amanda Griffith (Neé Reilly) & Jennifer Griffith at the school water pump.

way to school and hid them in a rabbit hole. It was too early in the year to go bare foot but as it was April Fool's Day we thought it would be a good joke but sadly the joke backfired, it was freezing and of course the master just laughed at us when we got to school. We couldn't wait to put them on again on the way home.

It was a long walk to school and back as I would have to walk down to the lodge to the Stackallan Estate on the main Navan Road and along private paths which belonged to Dan Leahy, the owner of Stackallan House. As my father was employed on the estate, I had permission to use this private road as a short cut through to the back gates of the estate and onto French Lane, which led directly up to school. For some time I made this journey on my own as my sister Betty didn't start school at the same time as me. She of course was a year younger and she joined sometime later and as my father's office was half way along my journey, I would always look out for him and wave if he was around. By the time I was leaving school however, there were four of us Reillys and four or five of The Feelys, our closest neighbours and great friends walking this route together. We had great fun and were always laughing and joking and never seemed to mind the long walk, even in the rain!

Some years after leaving school but here I am in 1952 with my father (centre) and my old pal, Noel Meade (right). This was a day trip to New Brighton after they had come to Liverpool for Aintree Races.

I really enjoyed school and of course I made many new friends. Altogether there were about 20 in my class one of my best friends was always Aidan Mead, who was six months younger than me. His mother, Rose Meade, was one of the school teachers and he had three brothers, a twin Padraig and brothers Noel and Fred and of course I was friends with them all. Aidan's brothers went on to work on the family farm, in fact Padraig had a gun and he and I used to go off into the fields together on many a night to shoot rabbits and swallows after school. Aidan however had a bike and used it to take himself off to the Technical College in Navan. He worked hard and eventually became a doctor. He used to deliver lectures from the Mater Hospital in Dublin and I used to listen to him on the radio years later when I lived in England. I used to think it was funny tuning into RTE on the car radio in a different country and hearing a lad I went to school with. I was proud of how well he had done for himself and that I actually knew him, above all however I used to think of the benefits of having a bike! I last saw Aidan at my mother's funeral in 1993, two old men together, laughing and reminiscing about those good old school days. Sadly, I last heard that he was very poorly with Alzheimer's Disease and that he was living in a Care Home in Dublin but despite that, I think of him often, he was a good friend.

Stackallan National School House was originally built in 1840, as per the marker stone embedded into the front wall, and I thought that it was a great place and full of character. There were two floors and when I was there, upstairs was for the infants and juniors and downstairs was for the older children and despite being almost eight years old, to my horror I was initially put in the upstairs class when I first started. Coincidentally my first teacher was called Mrs. Reilly, but she was no relation. I felt like a big gawk in that class and stood out like a sore thumb because I was older and much taller than everyone else. I think Mrs. Reilly felt sorry for me as she kept taking me aside to teach me how to read and write and I soon picked things up. She was a very big woman with mousy brown hair and she rode a bike to school. I liked her a lot because she was kind to me. On my first day, she took me by the hand and led me to my seat and I was grateful for that because I remember feeling a little embarrassed. I didn't really know what to expect of school or of my lessons but she showed me how to make my letters. I had my own school bag for my books and my own pencil. My English books and Gaelic books were like little pamphlets really and they cost me 2d each, my pencils were 1d. There was a big blackboard in the classroom but Mrs. Reilly generally went round to each person separately to show each one what to do rather than use it. I remember that we all had to copy what she did and then she checked that we got it right. I was in Mrs. Reilly's class about 12 months and I then went to the next room where Mrs. Meade taught. She asked me to write a composition once and I made a real hash of it. I felt dreadful but she was very patient with me and she showed me how to make figures and join letters together. She was of course Aidan's mother and I had great respect for her.

The downstairs classroom was where the headmaster taught and it wasn't long before I was allowed to move into that class. His name was Vincent Smyth, he was a bachelor and the son of a previous headmaster. I remember in his classroom that when the sun started shining it shone through the window and cast a long shadow on the floor. The master would draw a line along the shadow with chalk and we had to guess where the new shadow line would be at a set time. It was a good game and it was his way of capturing our attention and telling us that the sun moved around in the sky. The room itself was about 19ft x 12ft and all around the walls were maps of the world and different places that I hadn't known existed, as well as the obvious holy pictures, which were not small. They were huge. The picture that captured my imagination most however was one of a crow standing beside a glass jar with water and stones in it. "That crow has more brains than all of you and the infants put together," the Master would say and of course it was a long time before I fully understood why. He eventually explained one day that the neck of the jar was too narrow for the bird to reach in and drink the water at the bottom but because it was a clever and gifted bird it realised that if it collected enough pebbles from around and about and dropped enough of them into the jar of water, the water level would rise and it would soon be able to have a drink! The picture was there as a reminder for us all: If we think and work hard enough, we will be able to find a solution to any problem...'where there is a will, there is a way'. That story has always fascinated me and it was many years later when reading such stories as The Boy who Cried Wolf, The Tortoise and the Hare and The Lion and the Mouse, from Aesop's Fables to my children at bedtime that I rediscovered the story of The Crow and the Pitcher. I had never appreciated the origins of the story up until that point.

The school was heated by an open fire and Liam Feely and I would go to school early and get the fire going before the other children arrived. We would collect wood on the way, we would then clean out the ashes from the day before and place a fresh basket of wood by the hearth for the rest of the day. We were not allowed to leave the classroom until the master came in once the fire had been lit in case embers fell out of the fire and set things alight. The blackboard in this class was also used to record attendance, it had the names of each teacher and every day the numbers of children in each class were inserted and totted up. I remember there were exactly 100 children in school one day and I was surprised that there were that many because it was only a tiny place, not only that but where did they all come from?

The political problems of the country, of which we knew nothing about at the time, did not impact our community at all, not that I knew anyway. The clergy came together for the children's education and the school therefore served both Catholic and

65

Protestant. Everything was always very amicable and there was never any obvious trouble between the 'two sides'. The Catholics were in the majority in my school and we started at 9am as the first lesson was always Prayers. The Protestant children, I seem to remember there only being three, joined us at 9:30am, after prayers had finished. After that we read from books, Gaelic and English and even though I hadn't been there as long as everyone else, it wasn't much trouble and I managed alright. At dinner time we stood up and said the Angelus (Protestants included) and then the doors opened and we were allowed to play outside for an hour and have our dinner, which my mammy had prepared. For me it was simply a slice of homemade bread and butter that had been wrapped in newspaper!

After a short while, the headmaster would then summon us back in for afternoon classes and I really did enjoy his lessons. Amongst other things he taught me about The Industrial Revolution, Egypt, The Pyramids and The Vikings, and he drew wonderful pictures of the boats they travelled in. He always called me Sean rather than John and occasionally we would have to stand up in a ring and take it turns to read aloud. I dreaded him calling my name out as I hated doing that. It embarrassed me and I knew I lacked confidence back then, probably because I had started school later than everyone else and I knew I wasn't as good as the others. I didn't mind reading on my own, but not in front of the others and thinking on it now, I missed out like Hell sometimes by living down by the River Boyne. The house was too far away and I should have gone to school sooner. I would have liked that. As well as Gaelic and English, we studied Geography and History and we were tested on spelling, comprehension and of course grammar. We learnt Latin to help serve the Mass, Maths, we did some drawing too and of course punctuality and behaviour were always under consideration. With Mrs. Meade, the girls also learned to sew, knit and how to clean and wash clothes properly as well as how to prepare and cook meat, vegetables, soups, stews and of course bread and cakes too.

I can't remember what the exact lesson was on this occasion, but we all had to go up to the master's desk and talk about the book we were reading. I was always quiet and shy to go forward and one day the master said, "Reilly, sure you'll never leave your mother's apron-strings." Clearly he thought I wouldn't have the confidence to do anything but he was wrong wasn't he and I daresay my adventurous spirit would have surprised him. He would have been flabbergasted to see me years later stand up at Sunday Mass on a regular basis and read aloud in front of the congregation and to be perfectly frank, I even surprised myself. He asked me to write a biography once and I had to ask, "Sir, what's a biography?" "Oh Sean," he said, "Pretend you are a leaf on a tree and the wind has swept you away, write about your journey."

I loved that exercise and I remember writing a great story that the master was really pleased with. I described the trees down by the river by my old house and how the wind blew me right off into the water, taking me past the water hens and all the sights and sounds of where I loved best of all. I spent some time on that story as it really captured my imagination. I think he always managed to get the best out of me and I was saddened years later to hear that he had come off his bike and was found dead in the road on his way home from Navan. I'm not sure whether he'd been hit or fallen but the news shocked many.

The girls and boys were not segregated at school, we were all in the same room together although all the girls sat on one side and all the boys sat on the other. We sat behind three big long wooden desks that stretched across the whole room, five or six of us behind each one. The teachers placed a lot of emphasis on reading and writing and if you got anything wrong they'd hit you on the top of the head with a ruler. We all took our own bottles of milk to school every day and I carried mine in my school bag which was a brown satchel that my mother had bought me from Navan. It had a long strap and went over my head and one shoulder and as well as my milk, this carried my books, my pencil and of course my dinner. As soon as everyone went into class the first thing they did every morning was stand their bottles of milk around the fire and at dinner time, we enjoyed lovely warm milk but had to be careful that we did not burn our lips when the time came to drink it up. Should we need the toilet, we had to raise our hand and we had to visit a toilet block outside the school, but it was never a very pleasant place. Enough said.

Our teachers were firm but fair. I didn't really get into trouble and was generally well behaved although I do remember a couple of occasions when things went a little awry. During dinner time one day, a couple of the lads went to the orchard belonging to Mr. Rowan and we pinched some of his apples. I got caught because I'd pinched that many, my pockets were swelling and it was obvious what I'd been up to on returning to school. The schoolmaster soon collared me and sent me back to Mr. Rowan to apologise and return the apples. I just ran back and threw them back on the ground under the trees and ran off again back to school, I didn't go anywhere near Mr. Rowan, I was too afraid of what he might say.

I got into more trouble the day I put a dead mouse down the back of a girl's dress though. When I was on my way back from the toilet one day, I saw this dead mouse on the playground floor and as a prank I picked it up and put it down the back of Betty Thompson's frock. She was so startled she screamed and screamed and made such a hullabaloo that the Master made me get it back. "Now, smart fella" he shouted, "get it back." He went absolutely berserk and I was very lucky that he didn't get the cane out that day. It was a dreadful thing to do really but I was just a boy and looking back I think the master had a soft spot for me. I don't know what happened to Betty Thompson and I often wonder about her, I hope she forgave me!

Perhaps what I will be remembered most for though by my classmates is the day I broke the school clock. It was raining really heavily at dinner time this particular day and we were allowed to stay in the classroom and play while the master went off to eat his lunch. We were playing tick and running around when somebody brought a football out and we started throwing it around to each other. When it came to me however, I kicked it and instead of it going along the floor, it went so high I kicked it straight into the clock that was on the wall. Nothing was said and we soon settled back down to lessons but in the quiet of the school room the familiar sound of the ticking clock was missing. I watched in horror as the school master lifted his head to look at the clock and then take out his pocket watch to check the time. He demanded to know what had happened and I was so afraid I immediately owned up and said it was an accident. "Reilly," he said, "that clock has been there for 100 years and it took a brat like you from Barrastown[1] to break it. Well done." Once again I escaped the cane, he must have realised that it had been a genuine mistake but despite this, the story has been talked about by many ever since.

School finished every day at 3:30pm, in the main I'd walk off back down French Lane and back the way I'd come but that day I ran like Hell, I couldn't get home quickly enough. Most days as we cut through the yard of the Stackallan Estate, I would see my dad and stop and chat to him. My dad would often be waiting with the gate open to greet and chat to my friends on our way home from school and although my brothers and sisters stopped that day, I just ran on. I knew the others couldn't wait to tell him about my drama with the school clock and as I didn't know how much trouble I'd be

---

[1] *Barrastown is a short distance from Cruicetown*

in I just wanted to keep my head down and get home as quickly as possible. I used to go down to Hamill's Farm most evenings after school and do all sorts of odd jobs for him and even though he never paid me I couldn't get there quickly enough that day!

Hamill had five horses and a pony, loads of cattle that were out in the fields and they all had to be fed and have fresh hay. I did it because there wasn't much else to do and the only thing old Hamill ever gave me for all the years effort I put in there was a dinner of spuds and cabbage with a mug of tea on a Saturday. My father encouraged me to work there though and would always remind me that 'The Hamills had always been good to us' and that it was 'the right thing to do'. I spent most of my youth there until I wised up.

Typically, the time I did get the cane at school was the time I didn't really do anything wrong. It was the time we decided to idle our dinner time away by sitting on the wall in front of the school and there was about ten of us just eating our dinner and chatting and laughing. Right opposite from where we were sitting was a big field and one day Dick Flood, a local man whose children also went to our school, was ploughing it with two horses.

He never wore a watch but when he saw all the children pile into the yard to play at dinner time, he would stop what he was doing and make time for his own dinner. He would put a bag of oats over the horse's heads and he would sit down to eat his own sandwiches. This particular day, he pulled up close by to where we were all sitting on that wall and to everyone's merriment the horse's penis suddenly appeared, it was at least 12 inches long and of course being stupid boys we made silly jokes. It was nothing new to me as I had grown up doing odd jobs on Hamill's farm and of course we had had animals of our own for many years but others were not as aware as me that this could happen. Liam Feely took his bread out and started throwing it at the horse to see if he could hit its penis but when the bread ran out, he picked up some small stones to carry on with his game. What he hadn't realised however was that the master was standing right behind us and when he saw Liam Feely throwing the pebbles, he shouted and demanded that we all follow him inside. He was very angry and reminded us that Dick Flood could have been hurt if the horse had reared as a result of being hurt in a sensitive area and as a consequence he lined us all up and we were hit on each hand with the cane. This time I hadn't done anything directly wrong but I was guilty by association - another harsh lesson.

In preparation for my Holy Communion, the Parish Priest, Fr. Poland would visit the school once a week and question the children on religion. He was a very jolly chap, big and fat and he always had a job getting in and out of his pony and trap. He was such a happy man and he'd smile and laugh at anything, he used to think it was funny to crack his horse whip at you if you were too close to him as he passed you on the road. He never got me but I saw him catch plenty with it - it must have hurt like hell and he would just chuckle as he drove by. Everyone liked him though and many of the farmers would take him bags of oats in the winter so he could feed his pony, I guess it was their way of making a donation.

When he came to the school, he would sit on a chair by the fire while the teacher stood up by his side. We would have to go up individually to him and we would be asked questions about our prayers in school. I think Mrs. Meade must have prompted him about me being from the riverside and that I was a late starter as he used a situation I could relate to. "Now Sean, if you'd be falling into the river, got yourself in trouble and thought you were going to die, what would you do?" he asked. Of course, I had been instructed to answer, "Say an Act of Contrition Father," and I replied accordingly, which I always thought was a little stupid. I thought of my poor cousin Tommy Grace and wondered if his last thought was an Act of Contrition as he perished in the River Boyne Canal!!

The class made their First Communion together and it was a great event, I wore my best clothes and all my relations came and each gave me the traditional 1s/6d. I never kept the money, which because of my extensive family amounted to quite a considerable sum, I gave it all to Mammy but I did keep the set of Rosary beads that I had been given by the teacher. I remember that the altar rail had a big white cloth and that we were told on no account to touch the eucharist and of course we had been practising sticking our tongues out at school to make sure we did things properly.

I made my first Holy Communion in early 1936 in the chapel at Rushwee but this wasn't with Fr Poland, it was with Fr. Keegan who was totally different. He was a big brute of a man and once he threw a prayer book at me because I got a question wrong. Mrs. Meade, who was stood behind him was horrified and I watched her put her hand to her mouth behind his back. I wished I'd picked the book up and thrown it back at him but I knew that would get me into more trouble. I wouldn't care but I was also learning the Mass in Latin to become an altar server, I just wasn't paying attention and was surprised when he asked me the question. I never liked him much after that and even though I had been dying to get on the altar, mainly because it was a little bit of a status, I was quite glad when my father refused to let me do it when the time came. He said it was because I had to leave very early in the morning to get to Church before school began and unlike others that went on roads to school, I had to cross wet fields. This would mean that my feet would be soaking wet in school all day which would make me cold and miserable. I didn't argue about it and just told the master I couldn't be an altar server any more because my father didn't approve.

Rushwee Chapel is a lovely little chapel, hidden away off the road along a well-trodden path. I had been there with my mother many times after moving up to Cruicetown but it was far quicker for us to walk over the fields than go on the roads, so this is what we generally did. The first time I ever went I remember noticing that all the men were dressed up in their best attire and removed their hats on entering the church. I found it strange that they sat in the main body of the church, whilst the ladies and children, sat in the benches in the side annex. The ladies, who were also dressed in their finery, kept their hats on. When it came to the time for the collection box to go round, my mother gave me a penny to put in the box but I was fiddling with it that much that before my turn came I dropped it on the floor. It made such a loud noise in the silence and echoed around as it rolled and rolled and rolled under the benches all the way to the front of the Chapel. All the ladies and Fr Poland chuckled although I don't think my mother was too pleased. It has always been a special place to me, somewhere where I find great solace and I never fail to visit whenever I return home.

Visiting Rushwee Chapel

The ruins of the old Rathkenny Church in 2008

My confirmation however was held in the old Rathkenny Church, now sadly ruins, a couple of years later and me and my sister Betty made it on the same day. For some reason my parents did not come to the church but my mother had arranged for her sisters Alacoque and Rosie to take us down on the back of their bikes. They were obviously standing for us and it was enough for them to be there. It was quite a ride from Cruicetown to Rathkenny, it would have taken us at least 40 minutes to get there and once again, it was a day of great excitement. When we got back home we had a little party enjoying tea and cakes with our aunties, once again we were given money by our relatives and once again we handed it straight over to Mammy.

Towards the end of term in 1937, the master took us on a day trip to Bettystown, a small town on the coast. I was ten years old and many of us had never seen the seaside before - I certainly hadn't. I hadn't been on a coach either so I was doubly excited. As soon as we got there, we all raced to the beach and I remember that we all took our shoes and socks off, leaving them to one side while we all went off to paddle. It was a lovely sunny day and there was lots of merriment, splashing and larking about, everyone having fun. When it was time to leave, we all went to collect our shoes and socks and of course they were all soaked wet through. We had no idea the sea moved!

Breaking up from school for Christmas was extra special, not only because we were on holiday, but also because we had Father Christmas's visit to look forward to. The Christmas of 1937 however turned out to be a little bit different for me and one I will never forget. There was never much spare money available for many presents but Father Christmas did always bring us one small gift each and a few years earlier, I was delighted when he brought me a mouth organ. I played and played and played that mouth organ until I exasperated my father so much he picked it up and threw it onto the back of the fire. I was so shocked, not just by my father's reaction but also because I thought I could actually turn out a good tune - maybe I wasn't very musical after all. My mother soon came to the rescue however and fished it out of the fire, cleaned it up and put it away for me. I kept that mouth organ a long time, although to be fair, my tunes didn't really get any better!

One evening in late December 1937, I remember my father came home from work and my mother served up his usual spuds and cabbage at the table. To my great joy, she then announced that she was taking me into Slane to do some Christmas Shopping and I couldn't contain myself, this was also my very first visit to Slane. Strange now as I think back that I was ten years old before I went into my local village only three miles away. But times were very different then and I had no cause to go there. We walked along the main road and I held her hand all the way because it was pitch black. It would have been after seven o'clock and it was a good hour's walk but the shop stayed open late and I was very excited about my little outing. To my surprise, on this journey together my mother began to explain that there was no Father Christmas after all. "It's Mammy and Daddy that gives you things," she said, and after a little chitchat I soon realised that I wouldn't be getting the usual toy at Christmas. Instead, we were going to the shop so that she could buy me a new pair of much-needed breeches. It was sad that the magic of Christmas was over for me but I suspect money was tight and instead of wasting it on toys for me anymore it was important that I got something more practical. We went into Maken's, the main shop in Slane, which was attached to The Conyngham Arms Hotel, and she bought me a new pair of navy blue breeches. I then wandered around looking at all the interesting things in the shop while she got the groceries and toys for my brother and sisters. Of course she told me not to tell them what she had told me and I always kept the secret. I received my gift on Christmas morning like everyone else and of course there was always an orange and a little bag of sweets which we found at the bottom of our stockings and I still got those.

The house at Christmas was always decorated as my mother collected holly and ivy from the woods and draped it over the hearth, the windows and the Holy pictures of course. She collected enough to fill a vase that she placed on the table and she worked really hard at making it nice for us. The treat of course was the Christmas dinner which was always a delight.

School resumed and life continued without much incident until the end of the school term in the summer of 1940. I was 13 years old, and finally the day came for us to break up from school. The master got all the boys that were going to be 14 together and I remember him saying, "Remember Boys, to plough and sow, to reap and mow and be a farmer's boy..." I suspect he was reminding us that we would be moving on from school soon and that working on the land was generally everyone's calling. That's all that was expected of us and of course, that's all we thought ourselves but I have never forgotten those words that he shared with us that day. In fact a few from that class went on to do quite well for themselves, Aidan Meade became a doctor and Mary Brownwell, who was one of the Protestants, went on to win the Fáinne Óir, a gold lapel pin that was awarded to the most fluent Gaelic speaker. She won it in High School when she was a little older but she was the only one that I ever heard of winning it - it was quite something. Unbeknown to me at the time but the day the Master gathered us boys together and shared his pearl of wisdom about working on the land, was in fact my very last day at school. I never went back after that summer and as a consequence six years at school was the extent of my education and even that was interrupted with numerous days off to help my dad at Navan market, at home planting and picking the 'Kerr's Pink' potatoes he grew every year, at neighbouring farms at harvesting in the autumn and of course making butter with my mother.

July 1940 was also when my brother Patsy was born and I wonder if this had anything to do with me not returning to school. Was I required to earn a wage and start contributing financially?

5
Living off the Land

Whilst my mother worked every waking hour of every day at home, my father worked at Stackallan Estate, which was only about a mile from our home. That's how we knew Dan Leahy, the owner, and I remember that he was very fond of horses. My father however was employed as a cattleman on the estate and cared for all the cattle that grazed there, which were all bred for beef. It was my father's job to manage this part of the farm, collect rents and check daily on all the herds, regardless of who owned them. He was a well known and respected figurehead in the cattleman community and every morning and every evening he would walk off with his dogs and his stick and make sure that none of the cattle were sick. If he identified a problem with any of them he would notify the relevant owner and if necessary, he would ensure that the vet was called in. In later years, his dogs came home with him and there were two kennels outside the house for them but they were working dogs, we were never allowed to pet them, we didn't give them names and they were categorically never allowed into the house. If they came anywhere near the door, my father would raise his stick and say "Off you go" and out they would scoot. They were collie dogs and of course when I first got a dog of my own, it too was a collie dog and keeping the tradition alive, my son also has a couple of collie dogs. I like that.

The house at Cruicetown came with an acre of land that my father obviously had grand plans for right from the beginning. I watched him bring in cart loads of gravel which he used to widen the path at the front of the house. He also laid a stone doorstep and spent some considerable time levelling it all off. At the top end of the path and at the far side of the house, he built two animal sheds that had galvanised roofs and these were where the cows and pigs we eventually kept were housed. The small plot at the front of the house was for vegetables and flowers that my mother tended to and he planted damson trees all around the acre. He never had apple trees, just damson, just like we had down at The Boyne. Anyone was wiling to come and help themselves to the fruit as there were loads of damsons, bloody millions of them and of course my mother continued to make jam with what she could.

He got Paddy Doggert, who was the ganger at Crinnion's Farm, and two horses to plough up the back field before bringing the harrow in. When it was all ready he sectioned it off and planted vegetables in one half and sowed the other half with hay. He didn't have any machines for this and I can still see him doing that job. He wore a big white apron tied round his waist that he would fill up with seed and he would walk up and down, throwing it on the ground with his hand. After that, there was nothing much to do with it until it was ready and of course it was mainly used for the cows and pigs. Some years later, during the war, he had a go at growing wheat and once he had cut it down, he put it on a horse and cart and took it down to Hamill's farm where they had the thrashing machine. I remember that he got 11 barrels of wheat off the plot which he then sold, all apart from one barrel, which he kept for us. It was my job to take a bag of wheat to Rowan's Farm where they would make it into flour. I would go off on my mother's bike in the dark and I'd stand in line clutching my linen bag of wheat, along with many others doing the same. It was the only way we could get white flour during the war as it just wasn't available. There was as much as you needed to make brown bread but white bread was the favourite and of course it didn't last long in our house.

My father developed a mini farm in a way, I guess what you would now call a smallholding and my parents were always busy with one job or another. I don't know why, but we didn't bring the goats or hens that we kept down at the lock house up to Cruicetown. Maybe the smell from them was too bad, maybe my mother didn't want the hens in the garden scratching around her flowers and herbs or maybe my father sold them at market so that he could buy the pigs and cows that he eventually bought to take their place. He knew that he could get the same amount of milk from one cow as he could from three goats, with a third of the work involved and maybe Delia no longer needed the goat's milk. For whatever reason it was, my father got rid of the goats and bought his first heifer.

He was also the only working man in the area that had cattle of his own and it was not long before he had his own herd of 15 or so cattle and three cows. Each cow had a calf every year and he'd keep them until they were about two years old when he would sell them for a bit of money at Navan market. The cows produced milk once they had mated with a bull and produced a calf and we were therefore never in short supply of both milk and butter. My dad did not keep his herd at Stackallan House but The Hamills allowed him to graze them on a field opposite our house. I heard him say to many that he wanted to keep work and pleasure separate and of course I would not have been in a position to help him had they not been in the fields opposite. I daresay he paid for the

My son Martin feeding my father's cows c1963

privilege of having them so handy but they were close by and easier for us all too. The cattle remained in the field all the time but the cows were brought home every day for milking and were kept in our sheds overnight. In fact, the cows were kept in the sheds all through the winter, they were very well looked after and I often remember young calves who were too young to go to Hamill's field roaming around our back garden. It was my job to look after the cows when my father needed extra help and I would milk them in the morning before school and walk them back to the field in the summer months which often resulted in me being late for school. "Late again Reilly," the master would shout.

Cows were not kept by everyone and my father was quite a progressive type of man when I think back. He had more than most around us and many would come to us for milk and butter, all provided free of charge as there was plenty to go around. A byproduct of making butter, the buttermilk, was added to potatoes, bread or drank straight. Traditional buttermilk is not like what you can buy nowadays, it is much thinner and slightly sour and of course we only had fresh buttermilk on Mondays when my mother churned the butter. I loved drinking it and again, it didn't last long as neighbours would come with cans to collect from her as they too knew her routine.

My father was good with cattle, it was his job after all. When one of the bullocks up at the estate got sick once, he brought it home to help make it better. I'm not quite sure what was wrong with it but I remember thinking that he must be very knowledgeable to be able to do that. He dosed it up with homemade butter mixed with treacle which he made into balls the size of a tennis ball. He then rolled his sleeves up and forced the medicine down the bullock's throat one by one. I didn't ask many questions and just watched on in awe but the bullock was with us a few days until he made it better.

My father also bought a couple of pigs when we moved up to the new house, they were fed potato peelings, turnips from the garden and left over bread all mixed up with any leftover buttermilk. Whilst I tended to the cows, my brother Liam was responsible for the pigs. He would have to feed them, clean them out and put fresh straw down for them. Their dung was then mixed with the cow dung outside the sheds and this was used for fertiliser in the garden. When nice and fat, the butcher Mick Moore who lived nearby would come to the house and butcher the pig.

It was always a Thursday afternoon when Mick came to our house, it was his afternoon off from his job in Navan and I guess butchering my dad's pigs would have earned him a little extra money. True to form, when it was time to butcher a pig, I was kept off school again as I was required to help. My father would collect logs of wood that we had stored and make a fire in the front yard and then he would set a tin bath over the fire. He would get the fire going while I filled the tin bath with water and once full enough, my job was to then feed the fire with more wood until the water began to boil. Mick came about 2pm and with everything ready, he would unravel all his tools and stand outside the pig shed with a hatchet. My father would stand inside with a rope tied to the pig's back legs and he'd wait for Mick to shout "Send it out Dick" and with that, my dad would let the pig walk out into the yard. Mick would bang its head with the back of the hatchet and knock it out and then he would run for his knives and stick it down under his chin and we would all stand and watch the blood drain out. My father and Mick would then lift the pig up together allowing more blood to drain out before lying it on the waiting trestle table. The boiling water was then used to pour over the pig and Dad and Mick would then shave the pig of all the hairs. The pig was then left to hang up in the scullery overnight with a potato in its mouth and the last of the blood was collected in a strategically placed bowl. It was not unusual for animals to be hanging there, funny now when I think back that the girls would have a dead pig, dead rabbits and dead birds hanging up beside their bedroom door but at the time we didn't give it another thought.

The Saturday or Sunday following the kill, the pig was lifted off the pole in the scullery and back onto the trestle table outside. Mick would return and begin the butchering process. He would cut the head and legs off, the guts were removed and these went on the dung hill but he would wash out the bladder, fill it up with air and make me a football to play with. The pig was eventually cut up into pieces and we'd have what was called a bacon box to store the meat. White straw was spread on the bottom of the box and a quarter of the pig went down, then more straw, then each quarter until all cuts were packed away. There was room for 2 x 100cwt weights which were placed on the top to flatten it all out and the meat was then left for a couple of more days when Mick would return for a third time to start the salting process. The meat would be repacked into the bacon box, removed for a second salting and after this stage my mother would boil the two hams, one day at a time. Eventually we would have enough cured meat that would last for months and although it might seem a brutal process to some, as a country lad it was all fairly natural to me and of course the end result was always absolutely delicious, especially my mother's ham soup. I guess killing a pig that way wouldn't be acceptable today but that was the way it was for me and in reality it was quite a spectacle and all the young lads from around about would come and watch when word got about that we were going to butcher one of the pigs. No-one else butchered their own animals, just take them off to sell at market but my dad knew that he would get more for his money this way. He generally killed the pig in the late summer months and it would last us through the winter.

Dad would sell the cattle one at a time and with some of the money he made he would buy us all new clothes. I remember him walking into the shop in Navan with us and telling the shopkeeper that my mother could have anything she wanted and while we busied ourselves in the shop he would go to the pub and enjoy a quiet pint of Guinness. We would get decked out in new clothes just in time for going back to school, there was always excitement that day and at

My brother Patsy beside my father's first car c1945

the end of the shopping trip Dad would go back into the shop to settle up the bill. There were no buses on the road in those days but my dad eventually bought a little car and I remember us all packed into the back of it as he drove us to Navan. It was an Austin 6 and I daresay he would have sold a couple of cows at one point to buy it. Happy Days.

I watched the whole mating and birthing process through the animals we kept at home and in reality this was the only sex education that I ever had. When I first saw it all happen, no one explained what was going on though. I was about 13 when my dad asked me to take one of his three cows up to Rowntree's Farm. I had the day off school and at about 9am I set off walking the cow up through the lanes to the farm which was about three miles away but the cow was dead slow and it took forever. I didn't know why I was taking it there but duly followed instructions and asked for Mrs.

Rowntree on arrival. She led me off and opened a pen and left me standing there with the cow while she tootled off. She reappeared with a huge bull with a ring through its nose and she took the bull to the cow. I watched inquisitively as the bull sniffed around the cow before jumping on its back. In my innocence, I didn't really register what was going on, I just remember being intrigued. How naive I was back then, stood there watching the whole mating process without really understanding what was happening.

Late one evening and approximately nine months later, my father came to the kitchen door and asked me to go back out to the cow shed with him - he needed me to hold the oil lamp. I wasn't sure why, but when we got there I could see a baby cow lying half out of the mother cow. The two front feet were out first but once again, I really didn't understand what was happening - this was all new to me. There was no electricity of course and my father needed to help the cow and I needed to hold the lamp so he could see what he was doing. He kept stroking the calf and when it was fully born he took some straw to clean it up. All of a sudden, the mother cow smelt the calf, started licking it and we waited until the calf started drinking from the cow. My father explained that the first milk from the cow after the calf had been born was only ever for the calf, that it was called colostrum and that it was important for keeping the calf in good health - to me it looked just like thick cream. He cleaned everywhere up and removed what I now know to be the placenta so the mother cow wouldn't eat it and with the calf feeding successfully, he turned to me and said "Everything we can do is done, we can go to bed now" and we headed off back to the house. He was not really a talking man and he didn't spend a great deal of time educating us but just before we went inside he said, "You know John, the same thing happens to us," and for some time I really didn't understand what he was telling me. It wasn't until the lads at school were talking about it some time later that I made the connection. The whole exercise of taking the cow to Rowntree's Farm and watching the subsequent birth of the calf had been my sex education lesson and that was his way of telling me! For sure, I'd seen animals together, I just hadn't put two and two together - they say country folk know it all - but I certainly didn't!!

My father would go into Navan to trade at the cattle market for Dan Leahy and occasionally he would ask me to go with him. Navan had a big agricultural fairground at the back of the chapel and cows, pigs, goats, chicken and sheep were all available for sale. It was hectic and busy and I loved those days, the smells, the animal sounds and the farmers chatter. Being away from school lessons was good but the excitement of the market was far better.

He would often ask for my help in a whole host of matters and when I was only 11, he once asked me to go and collect a dog for him from Kells, which I now realise was about 20 miles away. It was another collie dog that was to be a working dog for him. I trusted my father implicitly and I knew I wouldn't come to any harm but when I set off walking to Beauparc station, I really did wonder what was in store for me that day. It was a good 45 minute walk and when I got to the station, a fella in a uniform came up to me. "Will you be John Reilly?" he said and when I replied that I was he asked me to follow him into the guards van. "You shan't be sitting in the train yourself," he said "You'll be up with us in the van." I climbed up and there was a seat there that I could sit on and I remember that we laughed and chatted all the way, through Navan and on to Virginia Road Station, the place where I was to collect the dog from. "Now you won't be getting off the train at all," the guard said, "The fella you'll be wanting will be waiting for you and once we have the dog, we'll bring you home." It was a great experience and it lasted most of the day. I just got on with it without asking any questions and just as my father and the guards had explained, the man met the train, handed the guard the dog and he brought it to over to me

86

on the train. It was still a great adventure and even though the dog was no bother at all, I held onto that lead tightly, especially on the walk home from Beauparc Station. When I got home, I remember that my mother greeted me with open arms. She must have been relieved that I was home safely but my father was still at work so I simply tied the dog up outside the house and waited for him to come home. He was delighted to see the dog when he came through the gate and that things had gone without incident. I felt very important and grown up that day.

After this successful trip I was given other jobs to do by my father and once he even asked me go to Navan Market with him as he needed help to sell a calf. It wasn't one of his own calves but there was something wrong with it because it kept sucking the tails of the other cattle. If this developed or if anyone found out it would reduce the cost of the rest of the cattle so there was no choice but to send it to market. Once again, he woke me up early to tell me that I wasn't going to school that day as I had to take the calf to the fair in Navan. He was going to join me later so it was a huge responsibility and he stressed that I was not to tell anyone about the problem with the calf. With no alternative I walked the calf the seven miles to the Navan fairground. I think a little boy selling a calf was the attraction and I think my dad was a little crafty having me there and so it wasn't long before a man approached me and asked if it was for sale. "I don't really know a lot about it, my dad's over there." I said and pointed him in the direction of my father who was trading as usual. He examined the calf and bought it anyway and he even gave me half a crown to walk it to his house. I was about 12 at the time and wasn't really sure where I was going but I did it. I just knocked at the house and told the lady I'd been asked to bring the calf. I don't remember how I got home, but I imagine I went back to Navan, met my dad and went back with him but it was another job well done for me and I was pleased with my contribution.

I enjoyed working with my dad and the odd day off school with him was always an adventure but when I was 13 or thereabouts I did a full weeks work for him, although I didn't get paid as I was really just helping him out at home. It was Spring and fierce storms had blown down scores of trees during the night and my dad had the job of clearing everything away but rather than let all the wood go to waste, my father and I spent this time cutting it up so that we could use it for firewood during the winter. He had a long cross cut saw and we cut the wood into 6ft lengths initially just so we could get it all home. After he had done all he could, he sent me to get the donkey and cart from Grandfather Harding and we then collected and loaded all the wood on to the cart. We drove across a little bridge over a river but my dad didn't think it was safe and so the next time when I was on my own, he made me go the long way around, which of course added additional time to the task in hand. For the week we had the donkey, it was also my job to feed it and clean it out - very different to going to school but I loved it. I much preferred being out in the open to being cooped up in the schoolhouse.

1940 also saw the arrival of the Irish Soldiers who came and took over Stackallan House during the war. Leahy had died and I think the house was empty but armoured cars and lorries arrived by the dozen. My father and I would watch the soldiers train and complete manoeuvres for hours on end and some time after my father and I had collected all the wood following the storm, we watched with amazement as several tanks crossed over the bridge that he thought wasn't strong enough for my pony and cart. "Now Daddy, will you take a look at that," I said and we both laughed heartily at our error. One soldier even asked my father to go courting with my sister Betty but my father refused of course and sent him packing. I imagine he'd seen Betty as she walked to and from school, I don't ever recollect her talking to any of them so I'm not sure what Betty ever thought of it all but she would have been very young at the time!

The soldiers were at the estate a good few years and we all got used to them being around. I remember hearing that the war had started. It was about eleven o'clock on a Saturday morning and all the family was at home. My father who had been out counting the cattle over at Stackallan Estate came home and was just about to wash and shave in front of the mirror in the kitchen when he put the radio on. We were the only ones in the locality to have a radio and all of a sudden when it was announced that England and Germany were at war, my father told me to immediately run up to our neighbour, Frank Feely, and let him know. It was big news of course.

I remember the radio arriving soon after we all moved into the new house in 1934. The man from Maloneys in Slane brought it to the house and set it up for us. I watched him climb onto the roof and attach one wire to the chimney pot and another one to a tree. As we did not have any electricity in the house we had to attach the radio to a special battery and every week we had to take it back up to Maloneys to get it recharged. With this addition to the family home, we suddenly became very popular and old Mr. Hamill used to come up every night to listen to the news and on a Sunday to listen to the football. When it was a big game, men would come from everywhere. They would sit on stools outside the house in the yard and Dad would open the window and turn the radio up so that they could all hear. Mammy and the girls were kept very busy making cups of tea for everyone.

My mother was the eldest of 11 children and lived up at McGruder's Cross until she married my father. She was christened Catherine Harding but my dad always called her Kitty. Even now I am in awe of her, how hard she worked and how she managed to raise a good family with very little. She worked unceasingly and her weekly routine rarely varied. First thing on a Monday morning she would make butter from the cream she had collected over the previous week. She had three big earthenware pots, which were about three gallons each and she used one for the morning's milk, one for the evening's milk and the middle one was always used for the cream off both. Every morning and night she would skim the cream off the top of the resting milk and as it was so thick, it was not difficult to do. This would then be transferred into the crock to be churned into butter. She would use a small wooden circular churn with a lid on the top that had a square hole in and she would attach two paddles that she would keep turning until she had butter. The buttermilk would drain from the plug at the bottom of the churn and she would catch this in buckets, some for us, some for the neighbours and some to feed the pigs. Eventually she would get a large block of butter that she would wash with fresh spring water collected from St. Patrick's well in Hamill's field and when clean she would add salt to make it more tasty. It was pure, it was bright yellow, it was lovely and above all, it was the best thing to put on our potatoes. It was a hard physical task however and she would often ask me to stay off school on Monday mornings to help her, which of course I didn't mind. She would regularly get 11 to 12 pounds of butter each week which she would make into small blocks with hand paddles and these were kept on a big board in the scullery and were free to use when needed. If any of the neighbours called for buttermilk they generally got a slab of butter too. While we were at school, she'd collect the potatoes from the garden and in winter she would cover them with straw to guard them from the frost. She would get a huge pot of water, scrub the potatoes clean and then boil them in their jackets and if we ever had any leftovers she would cut them up and fry them up on the griddle the next day with lots of butter. They were lovely and crispy and a great treat when we came home from school, especially if she added bacon and cabbage too. There would even be enough for the pigs too, they would get potatoes mashed up with the left over buttermilk from the butter. The vegetables for dinner whether it was cabbage, carrots or my favourite parsnips would always be in a separate pot and sometimes my mother would also ask Betty and I to go and collect some watercress, which grew wild in the river. She continued to make her own soda bread every day and the pancakes she cooked on the griddle were delicious and even better when we added the homemade butter. At meal times a big plate of jacket potatoes would be placed in the middle of the table and as soon as it was placed down, all the forks would appear and we'd all try and stab the potatoes at once. We would have the same meal of potatoes, bacon and cabbage most days, apart from on a Friday when it was customary to eat fish. Instead of the fabulous fresh fish we'd get from the Boyne whilst living down at the lock house, we would now get whiting from the fish man which wasn't half as good - one of the disadvantages of moving away from the riverside. Dinner was always ready for when my father came home from work and we sat and ate together in the usual way. The girls would set to cleaning away the table and helping with the chores while me and Liam would go and feed the animals.

My mother would set another day aside for washing, drying and ironing the clothes and bedding. We still did not have running water in this new house so for cooking, pouring on the butter and for making tea we used water from St. Patrick's well. The water was beautiful and cold and so clean, so naturally we always preferred that water to any other. After a pump was installed on the main road, we would go there for our water but we also had two barrels in the garden that collected rain water which we generally used for washing and bathing. To be honest, as we got older, I don't ever recall having a bath and Liam and I would just wash ourselves down in our bedroom using water in an enamel basin. It was that or a quick dunk in The Boyne to get ourselves clean. I do remember my mother would always wash our hair though and I'd hate it when she poured the cold water on to get all the suds out. I imagine the girls would have had baths in their room where it was private but I don't ever really remember going in there. I guess they'd make time when us boys were out of the way. We didn't even need water for the toilet, which was attached to the shed outside in the yard. There were none of today's comforts, just a basic wooden seat with a hole in the centre and a can underneath to collect everything and with nothing ever wasted, this then went on the dung hill.

Great care was taken with all the washing and ironing but more so with my father's shirts and I remember my mother drying all his collars on a little wire over the fire. Before ironing them she would spray them and the front of his shirts with starch so they always remained firm. Each of his shirts had two collars and it was usual for him to wear one shirt all week and then change his collar midweek to freshen things up.

On top of all her usual chores, my mother would continue to dust her bike off once a week and cycle to Navan for her weekly shopping trip. She'd return home with the usual sugar, tea, mustard to spread on the bacon and other household things. I don't ever remember my parents doing much socially as a couple but they both worked incredibly hard so there wasn't a great deal of opportunity to socialise. Occasionally they would attend a church event but it was rare as money wasn't really available for luxuries. They never went to the pictures, or out on day trips and my father certainly never went to the pub or anything like that, not until after we were all older.

My brother-in-law Tom Gray in the pub with my dad
Dick Reilly

6
Working for a Living

My schooldays were over before I realised but when it was time to go back after the summer holidays in 1940, my father said I needn't go back at all and that I may be better getting a job. School was never the place for me, maybe because of my late start as Betty, Delia and Liam all did well at school, but of course they all started at the right age, it was only me that missed out really. My brother Patsy refused to go once and we never found out what happened but something must have upset him. My mother asked me to take him and we walked together that day. I'd long since left school but my mother was worried about him and thought he may talk to me. He didn't say much but he went in no bother when we got there.

I wasn't doing much for Hamill any more, mainly because he didn't pay me anything and a friend invited me to go and work at Joe Brownhill's Farm which was a little further on from the school yard. Mrs. Brownhill, who was Scottish, was a great cook and in the September I was out in the fields working on the corn and she came all the way down the field with a can of glorious hot tea and homemade cakes. She had cups in a basket and those of us working sat down on a sheath of corn and enjoyed the treats she had made for us. I then started thinning turnips at the farm, picking out the ones that were no good and leaving the healthy ones to thrive. They paid 6d a drill so I was delighted to finally earn some money, all of which I handed over to my mother. I worked up to the winter months and was soon earning 10/- a week along with a free dinner, which I ate with the family every evening and we even had fish on a Friday, even though they were protestants - funny what sticks in your mind! Joe Brownhill didn't pay me directly though, I'd have to go to the Central Hotel in Navan once a week to see the gaffer for my wages.

My father however started getting concerned for me during the winter months. I had only just had my 14th birthday and although my walk home from work was similar to the way I'd walked home from school the past six years, this time I was on my own and it was always late at night after the day's work was done. I had to walk home down French Lane and across the fields to our house and it was so dark, there were times when I just couldn't tell the difference between the sky and the field and if it rained - well, I didn't have an umbrella! Around the time I would be expected home my father would stand at Hamill's gate and light his carboid lamp, holding it high and waving it around so that I could see which direction to walk home in. There were times when I was so cold when I got home it seemed to take me forever to dry out and warm up in front of the fire. I'd just have time for a wash, enjoy some supper and go to bed before an early rise again the next day. I never complained, just got on with my lot but unbeknown to me, my father had started asking around some of his friends for alternative work that would be suitable for me to do. It wasn't long before he told me that he had found me a job in the sawmills at Slane Castle instead and although that was the end of my days as a 'farmer's boy', I can't say that I was disappointed.

Slane Castle belonged to The Conynghams, or Lord Mount Charles as he was known to us, but the sawmills on the estate were rented out to a chap called Peter Butterly and that is where I was to spend the next five years of my working life. There was quite a number of workers on the estate but as I wasn't employed directly by the Castle, I tended to just mix with the lads from the mill although I did encounter others here and there as I went about my duties. The old Lord Conyngham often paid us a visit down at the sawmills and took quite an interest in what we were doing. He would stop and chat for a while, but not to me - I just watched on from the back of the workshop.

My new job was inside and of course this was so much better especially in the winter months and even though I was a general dog's body at first, sweeping up and making tea I enjoyed it so much more. I worked from 8am - 6pm Monday to Friday, and 8am - 5pm on a Saturday. My first job every morning was to light the fire and put the water on to boil so that I could make tea for everyone. I was also responsible for chopping firewood chips for lighting the fires up at Slane Castle and this is how I came to know Joe Smith the butler, Mary Browne the housekeeper and Kathleen Gormon the assistant housekeeper. Joe was a lovely man and Mary Browne was a tremendous lady, she was from County Kerry and when I went up to the backdoor, she would always ask me into the kitchen and give me a cup of tea with a biscuit or a piece of cake.

Slane Castle

There was I, 14 years old and being treated like a lord having tea in Slane Castle, sometimes I had to pinch myself.

I was in and out of the castle three or four times a week with the firewood and it was about a ten-minute walk from the sawmill. On my way though I would often chat to the other workers on the estate and my favourite was an older man called Arnie Lanney. He used to mow the lawns and trim the edges and although he wouldn't remember me as I was just a lad, I did often stop and chat with him as I walked up to the castle with the firewood. Old Lord Conyngham insisted that Arnie wore white pumps when he cut the grass so as not to damage the lawns and I always thought that this was funny. He worked with the Johnson brothers, Johnny, Geoffrey and Vesey who walked around pulling the weeds and making sure the drive was kept lovely and clean. I guess they were the estate gardeners, they were managed by a chap called John Heavey and they did a pretty good job between them as the grounds were always very well kept.

Joe Smith, the butler, wasn't a local man and he was about 15 to 20 years older than me, he was a thorough gentleman, always wore a black suit with a shirt and tie and I always felt inferior in my overalls. I used to think what a great job he had. He would tease me mercilessly about girls but it was good clean fun and when I ever returned to Slane I would always look him up. He took me and my family on a private tour of the Castle one summer in the early sixties and my daughter Amanda, who was about three at the time says that playing on the rocking horse in Slane Castle nursery is one of her earliest memories.

Mrs. Browne clearly held the authority within the house, she was always smartly turned out and was generosity personified. She would always sit me down and ask me lots of questions about what was going on down at the mill, who I knew in the village and what I'd been upto at the weekend. I was an awkward, lanky teenager entering an adult world and she definitely took me under her wing. She mothered me when I started work and I always enjoyed the morning walk up to the kitchens because of the welcome she gave me. She was a grand, bonny lady and her interest in me was genuine, I liked her a lot.

In the main though I worked with Jimmy Owen, Johnny Mooney, Jimmy Butterly (Peter's brother), Micky Farrell, Jack Brady, Oliver Hussey and quite a few more. I was just the little 'can lad' really but I eventually took on more duties and became quite proficient in my work. I loved working in the sawmills and even now

Michael Farrell and Micky Brien - colleagues from the sawmill

would say those days were amongst the happiest of my life. My mother would make me a packed lunch every day, homemade soda bread laced with her homemade butter and I don't know where she got the sugar from as it was always rationed during the war, but I had plenty of tea, sugar and milk to see me through the working day. I loved being back amongst the trees and I loved the smell of the freshly cut wood and soon learnt to distinguish one wood from another after it had been cut up. It was a good education and it was much better than stumbling my way back from feeding pigs over at Brownhill's Farm and although it was a two mile walk there and a two mile walk back, this time it was along the main Slane to Navan Road and much more manageable.

Soon after starting work at the mill, I was emptying the sawdust out in the yard when I saw two decent sized trout swimming up the stream. I followed them until they rested under a stone and slowly put my hand in and tickled their bellies lifting them both out one at a time. My days spent watching Barney McKeever poaching at the River Boyne had obviously not gone to waste. It didn't take me long to cut them up and cook them over the open fire before serving them to my new work colleagues for dinner. They were delighted with my surprise lunch and after this, I was well and truly 'one of the lads'.

I started smoking when I was 16 so most lunch times I'd borrow a bike and cycle to Mrs. Conlon's shop in Slane and get two packets of Embassy No 10 cigarettes, for me and Mickey Brien plus two blocks of tobacco for two other lads at the mill - I'd also pick up another packet of Embassy No 10 for Paddy Doggert our neighbour. I never paid any money over just collected the order and then distributed them out, taking Paddy his on my way home from work every night. Everyone would go to the shop on a Sunday after Mass to pay for the week's tobacco. Cigarettes became scarce during the war years but we still managed to get them here and there and of course I gave up smoking every Lent. One year I decided not to bother starting up again, but that wasn't until after I was married.

At work, I would catch the planks of wood from the machines once they had been cut by one of the more experienced workers, carry them outside to dry and stack them under the lean-to where all the wood was stored. I continued to work in the sawmills during the war and had moved up to operate the bandsaw. The largest saw was about 21 inches and there was a smaller one about 12 inches for cutting the smaller trees but just after my 16th birthday I cut my finger really badly while at work and was taken to Navan hospital. The doctors wanted to remove my finger but I wouldn't let them so they patched me up as best as possible and sent me home. I told my parents about the day's excitement and my father made me walk down to see the doctor in the village for further advice. He confirmed that I was right to have left it and the permanently bent little finger that I was left with became a 'distinguishing feature' as well as a constant reminder of taking great care at all times when operating the machinery. I learnt many new techniques and my knowledge of wood was developing gradually. I knew that elm, having strong cross-grained fibres, was the preferred choice for cartwheels, the stock and spokes were made from oak, whilst the outer ring, which was called the felloes, was made from layers of ash. After we had cut all the relevant parts, they were taken by the wheelwright and made into wheels. The spokes however were stacked up outside, covered over and left to dry out for two years before the wheelwright, who asked me to go and work for him once, could use them for the spokes. We worked hard and would cut all sorts of wood for furniture and even coffins, starting the process by going to select, cut and collect the wood before cutting it all into thin laths. We used a cheaper wood called deal for the coffin bottoms, elm for the sides and sweet chestnut, a soft wood which resembled oak for the tops. We received lots of orders from Slane Castle estate too, mainly for fences and gates and if we were to make a horse's cart, we would use larch. It was a thoroughly enjoyable time. Those working at the sawmill were never permitted to use the main castle entrance, we used a small gate to the side. The lorry, driven in the main by Oliver Hussey or Jimmy Butterly, would enter here and bring the tree trunks that had been cut down. All available hands would work together to unload the wood, there was a great team spirit and lots of merriment, such happy days.

Once it was clear that I was there to stay, my father cajoled an old bike off Vincent Moore, our butcher's brother. It was an old dilapidated thing but my father got chatting to a lot of the Irish soldiers up at Stackallan Estate and they agreed to fix it up for me. Vincent knew that it would help me get to and from the sawmill and as he no longer wanted it, he let me have it for nothing. The soldiers did a great job and before long I was cycling to work. I thought I was very fortunate as it made my life so much easier but I only had it about three or four months when Vincent Moore, who'd seen how we'd fixed it up asked for it back. I was disgusted but my father didn't argue - back the bike went, although I knew my father was also secretly disappointed in Vincent.

Having got used to the pedalling and my life being easier as a consequence, soon after that I went to Maloney's in Slane and bought myself a new bike. It had three speeds, a tail light, mud-guards - in fact I think I had a better bike than the boss. It was a belting bike, a bit heavy but it was all mine. I had to take my mother with me as I was under 21 and she had to be a guarantor but I set up a credit agreement and spent £17, paying back £1/7/8d a month for 12 months. I still have the receipt.

I worked for Peter Butterly until I was nearly 19, working my way up from being a boy apprentice to quite an experienced, valuable and loyal worker. Peter however was quite a mean employer and had not given me much of a rise since I'd first started work for him. I'd started on 10/- per week in 1940 and was still only earning 19/- per week, five years later, so I decided to hang back and confront him one Friday evening. "Peter," I said, "I think it's time I had a pay rise, after all, I'm a grown man now and doing as much as the others," but he just made more excuses about being a small firm and not being able to afford it. Needless to say, although he said he'd think about it, I never got a pay rise and so I mentioned to my cousin Willie Reilly that although I loved the work, I was far from happy with the wages. Willie was a foreman at Gerrity's furniture factory in Navan and he secured me a job working there for him and all of a sudden, from earning buttons, I was earning £5/12/- a week. I couldn't believe my luck, I felt like a millionaire. I joined the Union and finally got the 'going rate' and I was able to now give my mother £3 per week, keeping the rest for myself. I remember saving up and treating myself to a new grey sports coat and a pair of greyish/green flannels from a shop in Navan with my first wages, I felt like the 'bee's knees' and can be seen wearing them in the photograph Kevin took of me at the lock house in 1953. Very dapper!

Photographs of me as a young man

7
Spare Time

In my spare time, I did a lot of fishing. I had my own homemade rod, crafted from a hazel stick in the woods and even though my father had a proper rod and line for salmon fishing, I was never allowed to use that. I loved the solitude of being by the river bank and would regularly take myself off for an afternoon, fishing for perch, bream and eels. I would catch plenty of perch and eels but the bream always seemed to elude me but regardless of whatever I did catch, it always gave me great pleasure handing the fish over to my mother who would chop the heads and tails off, wash and skin them before throwing them into the frying pan.

Occasionally, I would meet up with a chap called Eric Brady who was away training to be a priest for most of the year. When he was home he would always come looking for the peace and solitude of the river bank too and we spent many a good afternoon chatting about this and that. He told me that it was his dearest wish to go out to the missions in Africa but once war was declared, he signed up to the RAF instead and became a padre in the airforce. I did hear that he managed to emigrate and fulfil his desire to become a missionary priest after the war ended. I enjoyed those lazy days fishing with Eric Brady.

I never watched football (gaelic football not soccer) or listened to it on the radio but my friends tended to. I suppose it was because I was never very good at kicking the ball so apart from fishing, I'd often take myself off shooting. There was never a gun in the house although my father did have access to one, in fact the one he used may even have been his, I think he might have just stored it elsewhere for safety. He would often go out shooting ducks and rabbits and take his gun but if I ever went out hunting, I'd either go with someone like Padraig Meade and use his gun or take a snare.

Liam Feely and I made a homemade snare once with some wire we bought in Slane and some old wood we found lying around and I remember the two of us having great fun as we took ourselves off one morning to a favoured spot in the woods to set it up. My father however wouldn't let me go out looking to see if I'd caught anything on my own that evening as it was too late. He agreed, after some persuasion, to come with me and off we went with a torch as it was going dark and we knew we would be out a while. When we eventually found the snare, I was disappointed to see that Feely, the bugger, had already been out and taken the catch. I was bit downhearted but we kept looking and soon found three or four more rabbits. We didn't always eat everything we caught as a lorry would come around to the houses collecting rabbits so I took them home and cashed in two rabbits for 2s/6d. I was chuffed and gave 2/- to my mother, keeping 6d for myself. I would also often go hunting with Eddie Brien, another friend of mine. His dad had a ferret and we would take that with us. It had a bell on its neck and we would let it go into the rabbit hole on a long piece of string and once we heard the bell going mad, we knew we had a catch. One day we took the ferret without asking his dad and led it into a rabbit hole. It was there for such a long time and we waited and waited and waited but the bell didn't ring. We were beginning to panic and didn't know how we would tell Eddie's dad that we had lost his ferret so we decided to dig down to see what we could find. We eventually found a rabbit but the ferret had eaten quite a bit of the back of its neck and it was asleep lying on the rabbit's back. This didn't bother Eddie at all, "Sure I can fix that, no problem," he announced and he took it off home. He borrowed a needle and cotton off his mother and cut up an old bike tyre which he stuffed into the rabbit and to be honest, he made quite a good job of making it look like it hadn't been chewed. So much so, he managed to get his money from the rabbit lorry and I often wonder what the person who bought that rabbit thought when getting it ready for the pan. I liked Eddie, he was dead rough and he was afraid of nothing.

During the war, I joined the Local Defence Force (LDF) with Liam Feeley and I was delighted to get my own uniform. Liam had joined up some weeks earlier than me and I used to admire him in his so I was really excited to get mine. My father wasn't too impressed with what I'd done and said I was "one of the fools in our family for joining the sodding army." He had grown up amongst the years of the Irish War of Independence and had witnessed first-hand the escapades of his younger brother Christy who had busied himself with their cause and then there was his older brother Harry who strangely joined the English Army during WW1. Christy and Harry both lived to be old men, but their fighting careers had obviously left a poor impression on my father. I persevered nevertheless and one night a week I went off to the schoolhouse where I received instruction with all the other cadets. After a few weeks training I even got to bring home a rifle but my father went berserk, in fact I don't think I ever saw him as mad in my life as I did that day. I didn't have any bullets and I showed him that I had taken it apart, removing the bolt and hammer but he was far from happy, reminding me all the time that there were children in the house. Feeling a little dejected, I wrapped it in newspaper and placed it under the bed. Every six months they herded us into lorries and took us down the country for practice, where lying on the ground on our elbows with the gun pressed hard into our shoulders, we shot at targets. Up until that point I'd not used anything bigger than the pellet gun I'd used to shoot birds and rabbits with, so to me it was all very exciting but my father had made his feelings well and truly known and without his approval, my enthusiasm for the LDF soon waned. I don't exactly know what happened to the uniform and

106

gun, they disappeared after I moved to England and I have no doubt that my father disposed of them somehow.

The LDF was my consolation for not being able to join the RAF, something I'd wanted to do since meeting Eric Brady, but I was under 21 and my father refused to sign the papers. As a consequence I had no part to play in the war and although I was disappointed with him at the time I have been eternally grateful ever since that he was so adamant I shouldn't fight.

There was a good social scene in the village in those days and as well as the odd game of football, which I was never particularly good at, some of the youth in the area went to a dramatic class. At weekends we'd go to a farmer's unused barn, hold meetings there and plan what we were going to do. Mrs. McGrath, who owned the local post office, organised everything - she would select plays, allocate parts for us all and above all, make sure we learned our lines. She got permission off the school teachers to run the plays on a make-shift stage in the school and family and friends from all around would come and watch. My parents, brothers and sisters came to see me several times and were quite surprised on one occasion when I sang a duet. The play was called "A young Man from Rathmines" and I sang a duet "Come listen to my story Molly Bawn", with a girl called Annie Smith!

Brian Og and Molly Bawn

(Brian)

Oh come listen to my story Molly Bawn

For I'm bound for death of glory, Molly Bawn

For I've listed in the Army where no more eyes can harm me,

Faith they'd kill me though they charm me, Molly Bawn

(Molly)

Wisha Brian, you been drinkin' now, you rogue

I can tell it by your winking, Brian Og

But you'd ne'er be such a villain as take the Saxon Shillin'

And to do their dirty killin', Brian Og

And shure what will all the boys say, Brian Og

That you've turned a red-coat h'athen, Brian Og

Go list so, if it please you, ach ya villian, do not tease me

Sure you'd drive a cailn crazy, Brian Og

(Brian)

'Twas yourself that drove me to it, Molly Bawn,

When you read my death you'll rue it, Molly Bawn

When I die mid' foemen wrestlin' where the balls like hail are whistlin'

Aye, and bloody bayonets bristlin' Molly Bawn

And the last words I'll be speakin', Molly Bawn

When me soul its leave is takin', Molly Bawn,

'An Grdh mo Croidhe mo Storn your old sweetheart Brian Ogn

For you his blood is pourin', Molly Bawn

(Molly)

Sure I done it all to prove you, Brian Og,

But I hate, oh no, I love you, Brian Og.

But keep up your heart, a Cara, for I'll buy you out tomorrow

'Tho I die of shame and sorrow Brian Og

And to think that you should doubt me Brian Og,

And meself so wild about you Brian Og,

Would let that thief Phil Dornan come and wed me in the mornin'

Faith you might have give me warnin' Brian Og

(Brian)

Oh I'm strong and hale and hearty, Molly Dawn

Sure I'm one like Bonaparty, Molly Bawn

And the divil a list I listed, for the Sergeant tried and missed it

108

And your mind, now you've confessed it Molly Bawn

(Molly)
Sure I'm kilt right out with schamin', Brian Og
It's meself that thinks it shamin', Brian Og
Since you didn't take the shillin' just to save your life I'm willin'
To get wed …..(they kiss)
……Behave you villain, Brian Og

Maloney's shop and Dance Hall at the rear

There were also numerous charitable functions to raise money for the school and I'd go along to those and of course the dances were plentiful. Barn dances and ceilidhs were common, a favourite of mine was the The Two Hand Reel, in which you had to dance with two girls but we generally went to the traditional English dances at Maloneys, a small venue at the back of the shop where I'd bought my bike. There was another dance hall in Navan that I'd go to occasionally with Liam Feely but we didn't always want to take our bikes and it was a hell of a walk so we generally stayed local.

I first sampled alcohol when I was working for old Hamill. He always carried a penknife with a corkscrew on it and I'd watch him open a bottle of Guinness with it, drink half and then pour whiskey into it from a bottle in his pocket, which for some reason was always wrapped in newspaper. He'd work some more and then have another one. Out of the blue one day he said, "Come on John, you may as well as have some while you are here" and that's how I got started drinking Guinness - thankfully not always with the added whiskey.

I didn't go to the pub until I was nearly 18. I'd go to a pub in Navan with Eddie and Paddy Brien but the The Conyngham Arms Hotel in Slane was always a firm favourite, along with Curry's, a local pub in the village which was run by two old ladies who were both spinsters. The place is still going but now known as The Village Inn and of course looks and feels very different. They would let us stay in after closing, which in those days was 7pm on a Sunday. I remember I was sitting on a bar stool and was with some of my friends before going to the dance when there was a knock on the door and in walked my dad! Jesus I thought and put my head down quick, of course I was under age and not meant to be there. He walked straight past me as clearly he wasn't expecting to see me there and when he wasn't looking I nipped out real quick and cycled to the dance.

I'd also often go to the Lyric Cinema, the picture house in Navan. I saw Gone with the Wind there with Maureen O'Hara and several films with Jeanette Macdonald and Nelson Eddy. They changed the film every week and we'd go and see most of them. They showed super films and it was a regular event meeting up there and of course there was always a lot of mid-week chit chat about who was taking who to the pictures at the weekend. Navan had a second cinema but it was a flea pit and no-one really liked going to that one so we stuck to the Lyric in the main. A fella down the street opened up his back yard to make a bit of extra money by charging all of those that cycled up 3d to mind our bikes. He was a bread man I think and I seem to remember that he'd had an accident and couldn't work the same so this sideline was quite a good extra little earner for him. He was a friendly chap and always had time for a chat.

I even went out with a girl from Navan for a while. She worked as a servant girl in a doctor's house in Dun Laoghaire and I got to know her through her brother, a chap I worked with. Her name was Bridie Booth and I can picture her now, she looked lovely, like a proper colleen with long black curly hair. It was about 40 miles though from my house to where she worked and lived so the journey would always take a while. I would cycle the seven miles to Navan, get the bus to Dublin and then the tram out to Dun Laoghaire. I never called it a serious association but it was nice enough and we would have lunch together and go for a walk. We would meet up once a month and when we were out at the seafront watching the boats on one occasion, I remember telling her that it was my intention to be on one of those boats one day.

I was also friendly with a girl called Maureen Sheehan who was in my class at school and Rose Hetherington from Oldcastle. I met Rose on the road one day in Slane and just got talking to her, she was a really pleasant girl. I found out that she lived and worked in the hotel and although I wasn't looking for anything serious we had some good times together. Leo Donnellan, my friend from school, was also friendly with Mary who worked in the bar so we socialised together as a foursome quite a lot around that time. Leo had a sister that everyone called Buzzy and I remember that she had black shoulder length hair with quite a severe fringe. When my granddaughter Jennifer was given a doll for Christmas one year, I announced that the doll reminded me of a girl 'back home' called

Leo Donnellan (left), Kathleen Doggert and me.

Buzzy Donnellan. After that my grand-daughter Jennifer named the doll Buzzy Donnellan and it always made me smile when she played with it.

I didn't tell either Bridie or Rose of my plans to leave Ireland, in fact I didn't really tell anyone and although I often felt guilty about that later, I just didn't want anything to scupper my plans. I thought that it was just best to keep things to myself. Soon after arriving in England though I did write a

letter to Bridie to tell her that I'd finally boarded one of the boats we so often watched together. I told her that I was sorry that I wouldn't be available for our next planned meeting and that I hoped she understood but I'd get back in touch when I was next home. Due to the fact that I never returned to Ireland to live, I never saw her or her brother Les Booth ever again although my younger brother Seamus sees Les every so often and sentiments are always passed between us.

Life was ticking along

Me with Mary (left) who worked as a barmaid at The Hotel and Rose Hetherington (right)

112

nicely. My eldest sister Betty who was only 18, was now married to Tom Gray and living in the Stackallan Estate Lodge House we all walked passed every morning on our way to school. She had a young baby Tony who was born in November 1947 and I remember that she was excited to be a new mother. Delia was 17 and was working and living over at Mrs. Mckeever's in Fenor, whilst Liam who was 15, was working for a sheep farmer, I think. Maureen and Patsy were still at school and then there was my brother Seamus who was born in March 1947 when I was 19 years old. Unlike the rest of us, Seamus was born in a hospital, up until then, my mother had only had home births but I guess because she was older this time, she had booked into Trim Hospital. When he was born, I cycled the 15 miles over to see both my mother and my new baby brother with Alaquoe Harding, my aunty. The long cycle ride paled into insignificance because I was so excited to see him. Until I heard the news, I don't think I even knew my mother was pregnant, which shows how naive I was, even at 20 years old. Betty never even mentioned it to me, which was odd as she was expecting at the same time - funny that, a mother and daughter having a baby at the same time!

Everyone continued with the same routines, mine being the daily seven mile cycle ride to Navan and my job in the furniture factory. I'd been there for nearly two years and the business was just getting back on its feet after the war but in early 1949, 12 of us were taken aside and finished up as work had slackened off. Being one of the last in, I was one of the first out, that was the way it was and I understood that. It was a Friday night and the news came out of the blue and of course my father had something to say about me being better off with 'Butterly'. I didn't want to work for buttons though and while I mulled things over, I decided to ride out to my Uncle Christy in Donore and stay for a couple of days. It was only about a half hour ride away on my bike and I remember taking my cousins, Anna and Betty, to the pictures in the evening. In a way, it was my first little holiday. I always enjoyed going to see Christy, he was my father's younger brother and I could sit for hours listening to the stories of his colourful past. Whenever I returned home to Ireland for a visit, I would always make time to call and chew the cud with him.

After my brief stay with Christie I was not home long when a builder came looking for me. He was building a cottage in the locality and he thought I might like to help out but I was only there a week and my hands started bleeding from carrying the bricks and just jobbing around. After about three weeks into this new job and totally out of the blue Peter Butterly knocked on the door of our house and asked to see me. He had heard that I was out of work and he wanted to persuade me to go back and work for him. "Come on John...carry on in the business you know best. Come back and work for me," he said. "Peter, I'd be delighted to come back, but it's a question of money. I won't come and work for buttons," I explained. After some discussion, the man who refused to give me a pay rise two years earlier now agreed to pay me £4 per week, not quite what I was earning in Navan but far better than what he had paid me before and so I agreed and went back to work for him, albeit a little reluctantly. It was far better than the building work but I was still a little angry that he refused to pay the union rate and to this day I often wonder if my father had asked him to call on me. I worked for him from June 1949 but I was now a union member after working in the furniture factory and I thought I may get into trouble for working for him and taking wages below the 'going rate'. Despite this, I persevered and was back working where I was happiest and this pleased me. The work at the sawmills was far better than the furniture factory, the wood was better quality and better to work with and I was back down by the river and amongst the trees, so despite the poorer pay, there were perks.

Clockwise from top left – My parents (Dick & Kitty Reilly), Betty & Tom Gray, Delia, Maureen, Patsy & Seamus, Me and Liam in the centre.

The Slane Castle sawmill hidden in the woods

8
England

Still feeling very dissatisfied, I made my mind up to go to England to look for work but I never told a soul. I knew my father would be too annoyed with me and my mother too upset, I was sure that they would try and dissuade me if they knew so I kept my secret to myself. My Uncle Jack, who was my godfather, had worked in the Metropolitan Police and lived in London for many years before retiring back to Ireland. Two other uncles, James and Harry Reilly, had settled in St. Helens, just outside Liverpool and I also had an Uncle Joe living in Bognor Regis. Several of my father's sisters had left home to work 'in service' and I knew that there were other relatives living on the south coast, in particular children of an Aunty Annie. Annie sadly had not long died. There were plenty of family living over there, I just didn't know any of them! I had met my Uncle James and his family as a little boy as they had travelled to Ireland for a holiday together in the early 1930s and I had got on well with his three sons, Gerald, Brian and Kevin. Gerald and Brian were a couple of years older than me but Kevin was my age and we became great friends. I remember the day I first met him and can see even now the mass of blond hair he had as a boy.

So with thoughts of distant shores in mind, I asked my boss Peter Butterly to do my wages early one week and explained that I had to go to Dublin 'on business'. Peter looked at me soft and I could see that he was thinking "Who do you think you are?" and "What business do you have in Dublin?" but I never explained further. My plan was to go to the Records Office and get a copy of my birth certificate which would enable me to obtain identification and the ability to travel. Even though my mother probably had the original certificate, I was too scared to ask her for it even though I was 22.

I eventually shared my plans to leave Ireland with Michael Butterly, a work colleague who was also Peter's nephew. I remember telling him one night that I was a bit fed up and that I was going to England to look for work. The Irish Government at the time wouldn't let you leave the country if you had worked on a farm and fortunately for me, none of the work I had done fell into that category. I had only done odd jobs here and there on neighbours' farms and I was anxious to move on so really there was not much to stop me. I felt so lucky as things could have been very different if I'd stayed working up at Brownhill's farm or at The Hamills. Michael was quite surprised to hear my plans but as he fancied a trip to Dublin and possibly venturing further afield himself, he tagged along too.

I'd been to Dublin a few times and I knew the place I was going to was along The Liffey. It was going to be a long day and

Michael and I set off early on the Monday morning, riding our bikes into Navan and parking them up for the required 3d charge. We then got a bus into Dublin and found our way to the Records Office. When it was my turn I approached the clerk behind the counter and explained that I had come for a copy of my birth certificate. "See that line of books up there fella, it's up there somewhere," he said. "You can tell me the date and I'll find it for you and post it on for 5/- or you can find it yourself and I'll post it on for just 2/- ." It was an easy decision. We searched for our own birth certificates, paid up and took ourselves off for some lunch by the Rotunda feeling very pleased with ourselves.

I suspect my family knew I was up to something as it wasn't often I turned out in my best clothes. They knew I'd been to Dublin but I never said why and no-one asked although they must have been curious. It was just a couple of days later when I was out in the back field working for my father. Every so often the thistles in the field had to be cut back to prevent the cattle from stinging their noses and I was working away cutting them back when I saw my mother coming towards me waving a letter in the air. She was obviously keen to know what it was and what I was up to, "Ah John, it looked important so I thought I'd bring it out to you." she said. "Oh I've been waiting for this, it's my birth certificate Mammy, I'm going to England next Friday." And that was it. That's how I told my mother about my plans. I don't remember there being any discussion or any arguments but the next day my father said to me quite calmly "Mammy says you're off to England, John. Will you think about it? They're all starving with the hunger there - will you not go?" "Ah, don't be worrying, I'm going for three weeks. I'm off for a look around and if I don't like it, I'll be coming straight back."

And with that I put my plans into motion. Coincidently the weekend before I was set to leave, my cousin Brian Riley[2] happened to visit our house. He had been born and raised in St. Helens in England but was working temporarily in Dublin as a glass beveler and decided to look us up. My mother had made a huge dinner as usual and Brian was just in time to join us. "I wish I had a camera," he said, "I'd take a picture of this dinner and show my mum." Food was obviously still scarce in England and Brian tucked in like it was the first dinner he had eaten in months. After dinner, we were all sat around talking and my father suddenly stood up and said "Come on boys, let's go and have a drink" and with that he takes the two of us to the hotel and buys us a pint. Brian was telling us about his job, and I got around to telling him that I had not long been finished up and that I was going to look for work in England. Brian was quite surprised but promised to write to his mother, my Aunty Kitty, to suggest that I stay with them and use his bed in his absence. He reassured me that his brother Kevin would help me look for work.

On my last day at the sawmills Jimmy Butterly, Peter's brother, bought my bike off me for £14 and I gave my mother some of this money so she could pay the balance I owed at Maloney's shop. With the rest of the money I made from the sale of my bike and with some extra money that I had saved I took off for England. All I had was £28, it was September 1949 and I was as 'happy as Larry.' I didn't know it but it would be nearly 60 years before I went back to the sawmills. I'd walked, cycled and driven past them scores of times but they are hidden from the road in the dense woods and out of sight to passers by. As they are also on the Slane Castle Estate, I wouldn't just walk in but I heard not long ago that they were derelict and beyond repair. However, my good friend Kevin

---

[2] My Uncle James Reilly, Brian's father changed his surname to Riley when he moved to England. The anglicised version of our name improved his chances of finding work.

Collins who works for Lord Derby on the Knowsley Hall Estate in Prescot, had connections and to my surprise, Kevin and Amanda secured permission for me to return to The Slane Castle estate on a visit home in 2008 and visit my old haunts. Henry, Lord Mount Charles and current owner of the castle, allowed us to explore the grounds and even though I couldn't make it as far down to the mill as I'd like, it was a tremendous feeling to be in the woods and the vicinity of my youth. Amanda and her family went deeper in to the woods but as it was wet underfoot and I was afraid of falling, I stayed near to the car and in the silence, pondered on my memories and happy days I spent there. They eventually made their way down through all the undergrowth to the mill and the small stream that ran past it, the stream that drove the huge wooden waterwheel attached to the side of the mill, the wheel that drove the machinery inside. They took lots of photographs for my benefit, some of which are reproduced here and to my great delight, the bandsaw that I operated as a young man, although rusted and full of cobwebs, still stands proud. We drove up to the castle and spent a short while there, the memories of yesteryear coming flooding back. It was a glorious day.

The afternoon I was due to set off for England, my parents were out. A friend and neighbour had died and they were off at their funeral. It was 23rd September 1949. Undeterred and with my plans in place, I set off walking, calling into Stackallan Lodge, to say goodbye to my sister Betty and to explain that I was on my way. I was glad that I could sneak off without having to say goodbye to everyone as I really didn't want any fuss but above all, I was excited about my adventure and much more relaxed now that I knew I was heading to St. Helens and that I had a definite place to stay with my Aunty Kitty. I had allowed plenty of time for walking the seven miles to Navan but Kevin Hoey, who drove the bread van, passed me by and picked me up. The drive hardly took any time at all and needless to say, I was in Navan way before I needed to be. I had my whole journey planned, I wasn't stupid and I wasn't taking any chances. I'd arranged to meet my cousin Brian in Dublin and have a drink with him before getting the overnight ferry to Liverpool and I was just stood waiting for the bus to Dublin when my dad rolled up on his bike all flustered. As he parked his bike up, my mother arrived on hers and my first thought was that they were going to stop me going. I was trembling slightly as he approached me. I didn't know what to expect but all he wanted was to come to Dublin with me. I was a bit taken aback about that but thinking about it now, I daresay they were very worried and maybe even cross, especially as I had taken off without any proper goodbyes and I often wonder if Betty got a message to them to say that I'd set off!

I hugged my mother, said goodbye and she waited until the bus was out of sight before she turned away for home. I now wonder what on earth she must have been thinking but at 22, I didn't think too much about that at the time. It was a relatively uneventful bus journey and my dad and I didn't say much to each other - quiet in our own thoughts. I told him that I was meeting Brian at the column in O'Connell Street and reassured him that I would be fine but after meeting up with him, we spent the afternoon chatting and talking until it finally came time for me to go. We all made our way across to the port where the ship was docked and finally I said "Ta ra Dad, I'd better be off now," to which he replied "Look after yourself son and whatever you do, keep clear of funny women and never forget your religion. Take care John." Sound advice! He shook my hand and then to my surprise he gave me a hug before finally waving me off. I made my way onto the boat and waved once more. It left Dublin at 10pm but despite the late hour it was still daylight. It was late September and a lovely warm summer evening, there were lots of lights on the boat and plenty of men drinking beer and girls dancing, it was a great atmosphere. I had a very small green suitcase that my Uncle Christy had given me so I couldn't take much, just a couple of shirts and some working clothes. I was surprised to see that the bottom of the boat was full of cattle and even more surprised that we had to drop the cattle off first at Birkenhead before passengers could alight at The Pier Head, in Liverpool but after grabbing snippets of sleep here and there on the overnight crossing, I was up early in the morning and out on deck as the boat sailed into the port. It was a memorable sight and I enjoyed taking it all in. My first impression however was not so much about the grand buildings we slowly sailed past on our way up the River Mersey but the extent of the damage that was still apparent after the war and specifically the number of ship wrecks that were still protruding from the water. Once docked, I remember thinking, "This is it - here we go," and stepped off into the unknown with my case in hand.

Brian had not given me any instructions about getting to his house from Liverpool but I saw some buses parked, asked where they were going and when I was informed it was for Lime Street Railway Station, I got on. It was only a short journey and I was naturally inquisitive looking this way and that and I remember thinking that the City Centre seemed exceptionally busy considering it was only 7am in the morning but I guess everyone was making their way to and from work. At Lime Street station, I asked for the next train to St. Helens and as I had just missed one, I sat myself down on a bench and waited. I saw a fella selling teas and sandwiches and bought what I now know to be egg and cress sandwiches, at the time however my main thought was "Bloody hell, they eat the shamrock over here." I sat under the big clock and eventually got on the 8am train to St. Helens, making sure that I got a window seat so that I could read the names of each station and therefore know where to get off.

Brian's instructions after arriving in St. Helens were very clear and I knew that I had to walk from the train station to the old bus terminus and take either the number 7 or number 8 bus to a place called Toll Bar. Once settled on the bus, I leant forward and asked the two ladies sitting in front of me if they'd mind telling me when I got to Toll Bar as I didn't really know how far I had to travel. "Yes Love - of course we will" one replied, which took me back a bit as I couldn't understand why she called me "Love" she didn't know me and I was not accustomed to that 'term of endearment' from a stranger at home. I got off the bus at the Welsh Chapel on Lugsmore Lane as directed, found Leslie Road, walked right up to the top of the hill to number 99 and knocked and waited. Aunty Kitty opened the door and exclaimed with delight, "John, come in, come in, I've been waiting for you".

Brian had mentioned that food was scarce in England since the war and so I handed over a small hamper that I had put together for her and another one that Brian had asked me to take too. She was completely overjoyed to see the tins of fruit, tins of soup and large lump of bacon and rashers I had brought over with me and she was soon mothering me and making me feel at home.

My cousin, Kevin, no longer sporting the very blond hair he had as a child, came scurrying down the stairs in his pyjamas. I'd left my other cousin Brian behind in Dublin, sadly Gerard, who was the eldest, had been killed whilst training to fly planes in Canada for the war and my Uncle James had long since died. The morning I arrived in St. Helens was a great morning, with lots of excitement and my first thought was how well-dressed Aunty Kitty was. She had grey mousey hair with lots of curls and waves and I also remember thinking that she was not white skinned like my mother, she was quite olive skinned but despite all that, the thing that I noticed above anything else was that she had lots of whiskers on her chin! We all sat together in the tiny kitchen at the back of the house whilst she opened up the bacon and made Kevin and I some bacon and cheese on toast, which I wolfed down. I thought my house was small but this place was tiny. My first priority however was to visit the Post Office and send a telegram to my mother to let her know that I had arrived safely and make an application for some ration books which I handed straight over to Aunty Kitty. It was Saturday morning and after more chit chatter and copious cups of tea, Kevin decided to take me to see 'Saints' play Rugby. 'Saints', I later found out was the local Rugby League team of St. Helens and Kevin was a fan! I wasn't a sporting man and I hadn't had much sleep but I didn't want to offend him so we trundled off firstly to The Sefton Pub in St. Helens town centre and then the rugby ground at Knowsley Road, which wasn't too far away. It was the first time I'd seen Rugby, I didn't understand the rules so it didn't really mean much to me, but Kevin was very keen and he went regularly to watch home games. I do remember being impressed with a chap called McCormick who was an exceptionally fast runner and somebody by the name of Prescot who was a heavy lump of a man. I met him years later when he brought the winner's trophy to the school where my wife Rita taught.

I didn't waste too much time in looking for work and spent the early part of the following week, walking around St. Helens asking for jobs as a wood machinist. No-one seemed to be taking anyone on and so Kevin suggested going further afield to Liverpool, which was approximately ten miles away from where I was staying. Kevin was working as a joiner at the time and through his connections, he knew of a few furniture shops that he thought might be worthy of a try, so we headed off together on the bus. We went along Prescot Road, got off at Jubilee Drive and walked along Kensington where there were numerous furniture shops. At first I didn't have any luck as they mainly seemed to be upholstery shops but finally someone directed me to Freeman's Furniture Business on Holborn Street. "Tell them, I sent you," he shouted after me as we left his shop and marched on with a spring in our step.

Eventually we came across this little factory, hidden away behind big black doors but I could hear the machinery going and whilst Kevin loitered outside somewhere, I approached the only man in the room and asked if I could speak to the foreman. I later learned that the man I spoke to was called Jim Swanson and he was as bald as a coot when he took his cap off. I told him I was looking for work so he asked me to wait and disappeared off upstairs reappearing five minutes later with Charlie, who I later learned was the boss's son. I came to know them both very well. Charlie explained that they couldn't produce products quickly enough for the upholsterers and the prospect of work was promising so he took me up to the bandsaw and asked me to demonstrate what I knew. He quizzed me further about all the types of machines I'd worked on and so I showed him that I could work the planing machine and I even produced a bit of a spindle. He wore a long brown coat and I remember thinking that he looked really smart and I was keen to impress him as I thought I'd like to work there. I explained my situation, that I'd travelled over from Ireland the previous week and from St. Helens that morning and even admitted to being a bit lost. After chatting some more, I was delighted when he confirmed that I could start work for him the next morning and was even more impressed when he insisted that I was not to worry if I arrived late. He was content to allow me some flexibility whilst everything was so new to me and I was simply flabbergasted that an employer could be so generous. As we headed back to St. Helens I told Kevin all about Charlie and confided in him that if everything worked out as well as expected it was likely that I might stay. Kevin joked that I had fallen on my feet and commented that I seemed to have the 'Luck of the Irish'. With time - I was inclined to agree with him.

It was an early start the next day as the bus journey was an hour long and I wanted to impress by trying to get there as early as possible, apart from anything else I was really excited to start on this new adventure. I started off making wooden chair legs and arms and soon settled in. Jim Swanson took me under his wing and even though he was a lot older than me, we got on very well together. I was also introduced to Ernie and Billy O'Neill, brothers who worked upstairs in the assembly room and after some time there, we all became great friends. Had I lived nearer to work I daresay, we would have socialised more together but after a hectic working day, I was just ready to get home. Everyone finished at 5pm and during the first week, I'd stand at the bus stop for an hour and a half before I could get onto one of the overcrowded buses and on top of the long bus rides to and from home, my working day was proving to be longer than expected. I was chatting to the lads at work about the situation and once again was surprised by Charlie who suggested that I work a couple of hours overtime at the end of each day so that I could catch the 6:50pm bus and thus avoid the crowds. My normal wages were £6/12/- a week and an extra £2 per week overtime, made this an offer I couldn't refuse.

In November there was a Catholic Holiday so I got up extra early so that I could go to mass at Sacred Heart RC Church opposite where I worked. I was surprised to see Billy and Ernie at the same mass as I didn't know they were Catholics and when I was coming out of mass they came running after me and made quite a fuss of seeing me there. From that day on I felt we were more like brothers than work mates and a camaraderie developed between us that was second to none. When Christmas arrived, I was staggered to receive a £10 Christmas Bonus from Charlie, I had only been there a couple of months and found it incredulous that I was treated exactly the same as everyone else. I bought my first watch with that £10, a watch I still have today, however sadly it is no longer in working order. Despite not having much joy in getting it fixed I can't bear to part with it.

I'd write home every blue moon and tell everyone my news, where I was living and what I was doing but it was Aunty Kitty who wrote regularly and reassured my mother that I was doing alright and more importantly that there wasn't anything for her to worry

Patsy and Delia at home - Winter 1949

about. Just like in school, I was shy of writing especially in front of Kevin and Aunty Kitty so I didn't do it as often as I should and by the time I got home from work, Kevin was waiting eagerly for me to go out with him but in hindsight, I think I perhaps should have tried harder. I went home for Christmas that first year, my little suitcase full of gifts for everyone. It was such a cold winter and the boat was freezing. It was wonderful to be back home and walk into the warmth of the open fire in my parents' kitchen and allow my mother to make such a fuss of me. The familiar smell and feel for my own home was something special and to see the open fire, the house all ready for Christmas and so many welcoming and smiling faces was a pure joy. Almost immediately, a hot cup of tea and some home-made cake was thrust in my hand and I was made to sit down and tell everyone all about my new beginnings. I remember Seamus jumping around and getting over excited but overall, it was a cosy, warm evening in my own home, surrounded by my own family and I was happy to be back. The following morning I went down to Hamill's yard to say hello and the two old farmers were stripped down to the waist and washing themselves from the huge trough that the horses would drink from. It was freezing cold and their skin appeared blue - they must have been as tough as old boots! After a week at home however it was time to head back to Liverpool and my new routine.

After working at the Liverpool furniture factory for two years, Charlie asked me if I knew anything about felling trees, "I want you to come to my house and take down a tree that's blocking the light. I don't want you to hit the neighbour's greenhouse though, can you do it?" Of course this was not a problem to me and I made my way over to Oak Road in Aigburth where he lived, climbed up, removed the branches, nibbled at the bottom and it came down beautifully. He was so chuffed that he got all his neighbours to look at my work. I was well supplied with tea, biscuits and sandwiches but as I did it in working hours, I didn't get paid for the work, which was what we agreed. I was just happy that I was able to help and that he respected me enough to invite me to his home.

I was perfectly happy working hard and enjoying the adventure of a lifetime. I had a good wage, a good roof over my head and the social scene was far better than at home. Brian, Kevin and I always socialised together, we became great friends. After Mass at Portico Church on a Sunday we would often walk down Red Rocks, a small sandy pathway and short cut to one of our regular pubs, The Griffin in Eccleston. Brian would stand and watch the fellas playing golf as we passed the golf course. He was always interested in learning how to play and it came as no surprise when I heard that he had joined the golf club years later. Occasionally we'd walk up to The Bottle and Glass in Rainford which was quite a stretch but in the main we stayed fairly local and on a Saturday night we'd generally be found in the bar of The Fleece Hotel – sadly no longer standing, The Sefton or The Market – all well known drinking venues in St. Helens. Brian didn't join in as much and so by default I became more friendly with Kevin and although we would take ourselves off to dances, Kevin would never dance. He was a very shy young man but we all danced back then, especially if we'd had a few beers. After a few weeks of watching Kevin just standing watching I suggested he go to a dance school and so we enrolled at The Maida School of Dancing to help him improve. It was just a big room in a big house but Kevin didn't seem to enjoy it as much as me. He kept looking at his feet so the teacher took him under her wing and helped him along. I was used to doing a fair bit of dancing back home so it was easier for me and I really enjoyed those classes.

9

Rita

My plan to stay in England for three weeks soon went awry and before I knew it, I'd been in St. Helens six months. It was February 1950 and I was perfectly happy working hard and enjoying the adventure of a lifetime. This particular Saturday, Brian, Kevin and I decided to enjoy a couple of pints at the The Fleece Hotel before taking ourselves off to a Valentine's dance at Sacred Heart Church Hall, St. Helens. It was really busy when we got there so the three of us just stood about chatting and as I scoured around the room, I decided to get a young girl, who I thought was nice looking, up to dance. I left the other two talking to each other and took myself off. The girl's name was Mary Banks and after a good chat whilst dancing, I found out that she was a school teacher. I enjoyed my time with her, thanked her for the dance and then went back to find Brain and Kevin. Before long I decided to go off for another wander and left them alone again and this time as I walked across the line of chairs against the back wall, a young lady, who was already sitting on a man's knee, suddenly smiled at me. I was a bit taken aback but I approached her and asked her for a dance.

When we first got up, there was only the two of us on the dance floor and I felt a little conspicuous but before long others soon joined in. I found out that her name was Rita and she was at the dance with her cousin Joan Green and Joan's boyfriend Ray Johnson - the man whose knee she was sitting on. We had a great time chatting and dancing and after meeting Rita, I didn't end up going back to Kevin or Brian at all that night. At the end of the evening, I politely asked Rita if I could take her home and was delighted when she agreed. We walked to the bus stop and I remember saying "I'm a right one to take anyone home, as I don't

1950 - Rita and I

really know where I live myself." We continued to laugh and chat on the bus journey home and Rita reassured me that she would help me find my way back to where I knew.

We got off the bus at Prescot and walked through the small town centre to her house in South Avenue. It wasn't a familiar place to me but it struck me as being a decent place with many good shops and Rita could tell me about this and that as we walked by. When we got to her front gate and said our goodbyes, I asked if I could see her the next day. We agreed to go to the pictures in St. Helens and made plans. I was no longer living with my Aunty Kitty as Brian needed his bed back when he returned from working in Dublin but I had moved in with my Aunty Kitty's sister, who I called Aunty Annie. Annie lived with her husband Jack Seed and their daughter Renee at 15 Willow Road and for a short time they became my new family. After dropping Rita off at her home she explained the easiest way for me to get back to St. Helens and by the time I got home it was one o'clock in the morning. I remember the streets being very quiet and after letting myself in I crept up the stairs, taking great care not to wake anyone up. The next morning, Brian and Kevin couldn't wait to hear all about my 'romance', they came rushing down to see me at Aunty Annie's and I couldn't wait to tell them that I was meeting up with Rita again that evening. I was really looking forward to seeing her again and that night when I got on the bus to go and meet her, to my surprise, who was sitting on the same bus? None other than my lovely Rita. She was all dressed up in a brown tailored suit and a cream blouse and when I sat myself down next to her she offered me a cigarette. We went to the pictures in St. Helens as planned but for the life of me, I can't remember what film we went to see. I'm sure she would have known, but to me it wasn't of any consequence. I was just so happy to have her company.

Both Auntie Annie and her husband Jack, spoiled me dreadfully. They were a lovely couple and when we were just sitting around chatting Aunty Annie would often say "Come on, you must have had a busy day - lie out!" and then she would cover me over with a shawl. I was really mollycoddled by them and every evening when I got home from work, my dinner was always ready and resting over a pan of hot water. They were non-catholics and Aunty Annie was very involved in her own church, St Johns in Thatto Heath and as she was often out when I got home from work, Uncle Jack would serve it up for me - he really was a smashing man. Saturday mornings however were my favourite time with them, as Aunty Annie would take some plates to the chip shop and leave them there until lunch time. This was something new to me and I couldn't wait for her to nip back out at lunchtime to collect our dinner on red hot plates. We'd all dive into masses of chips which were served with plenty of bread and butter, I'd never known anything like it and it was such a treat. "Leave that plate there, I'll move it and you go off and meet Rita," Auntie Annie would say. I loved that routine, she was so good to me and I'd shout my goodbyes as I made a dash for the door and the bus to Prescot. I was exceptionally happy living there, I had my own key and I was free to come and go as I pleased. I was always respectful if I was late and tried not to disturb anyone if they were in bed when I got home. I never forgot the family's kindness and regularly took my own little family back to meet Annie,

Jack and their daughter Renee, years later.

After that first night out to the pictures, I went to meet Rita every evening. I'd get the bus home from work, have my dinner, freshen up and get another bus back out to Prescot. I was very careful not to overstep the mark and I took the courtship slowly. We would go for walks along the main road and I got to know her very well. Two to three weeks went by and she asked what I did on a Saturday afternoon, "Not much," I replied, "I wander around St. Helens and the market." "Come to me and we'll go to Liverpool," she said. "We'll go the pictures and get something to eat" so I told Auntie Annie that I wouldn't be home for evening dinner on Saturday and that was the beginning of a routine that we followed for some time.

It was only after knowing her for four weeks that she told me that she was a teacher and that only came about after we passed three girls whilst we were walking down Knowsley Lane, not far from her home. It was a lovely, clean, bright sunny evening and the girls were fooling around with a load of Americans soldiers who were stationed at the Burtonwood RAF airbase several miles away. As we walked past them, one by one the girls said,

"Evening Miss,"

"Evening Miss,"

"Evening Miss."

I wondered what was going on and it was only then that Rita told me she was a teacher and they were in her class at school. I remember Rita laughing when in all sincerity I said, "I'm not sure there's much you can teach those lasses."

Rita was a lovely girl, very sincere and honest and she opened up to me fairly early on in our relationship, setting the boundaries and ensuring that I understood her commitment to marriage. I think it was her way of 'warning me off' but I wasn't like that, I had an enormous amount of respect for Rita and I wasn't

135

going to spoil what we had. In addition, I didn't want to make any mistakes and be forced to stay in England if there came a point when I wanted to return home! I for one, wanted to take things slowly and steadily.

Before long, Rita invited me into her house to meet her mother and I remember being very impressed by her. She was a lovely lady, beautifully dressed and her house was spotlessly clean. She was such a kind looking lady and I took to her immediately. "Very pleased to meet you maam," I said. She seemed happy to say hello and as she was only small and I so tall, she had to bend her head right back to look up at me. Rita's dad was a butcher and worked Saturday mornings so I didn't meet him on that occasion, but overall I remember thinking it was a pleasant and comfortable meeting with her mother and that pleased me. Rita and I said our goodbyes as we set off on our routine trip into Liverpool and true to form, we'd get off the bus at Lime Street and either go to the pictures, wander through the shops or enjoy a fish and chip supper at a little restaurant that we used to frequent. It wasn't long after that that I met Tom Moran, Rita's father. He'd heard that I was Irish and had his concerns but he welcomed me into the family with ease - after all, The Morans originated from the North West of Ireland and earlier generations had left Ireland during the 1850s, just like my own family. Tom and I got on exceptionally well all through our lives, we shared the same values and beliefs. When I reflect, I couldn't have asked for better in-laws.

During the summer of 1950, I went home to Ireland for a week's holiday and my cousin Kevin travelled with me. Kevin had great memories of the holiday he had enjoyed there in the early 1930's as a small child and he couldn't wait to revisit Castlefin Lock House, the house where I and both our fathers were born. We spent lots of time down there that week, we walked up and down the ramparts and enjoyed the flow of the water, watching the water hens and life along the river bank. Kevin also took the photographs of me outside the old lock house, that I now cherish dearly. Like me, Kevin loved being beside the river, he was fascinated by the size of the small lock keeper's cottage and used to chat about what life must have been like for our family living down there. It is a strikingly beautiful place, even now when all over grown with ivy and brambles and I never have nor ever will take the beauty of where I grew up for granted. I'm proud to say that I was born on the banks of the River Boyne and I'm proud to show people the old family home, buried deep and hidden amongst the trees of the valley. I

think it's just the isolation and simplicity of it all that surprises those that visit, it renders everyone into silence as they digest where they are, as they contemplate the lives of those

Revisiting Castlefin Lock House
1953

that lived and died there and of course how beautiful it would be if it were all as it should be. The programme to upgrade the canal, the locks and towpaths around where I was born will not be complete in my lifetime, I am not sure it will be complete in my children's lifetime, but my grandchildren Jennifer, Martha and Edward should be able to revisit the restored site. With luck, it will look a lot better than it did when they all visited in 2013. It was unthinkable for me to try and venture down with them but I was delighted that they all

137

spent some time down there. Who would have thought that after we vacated the house in 1934, it would still be there for another two generations of Reillys to visit.

Back in 1950, Kevin and I shared what used to be the girls' bedroom that summer and although nothing really had changed since I had left, I did notice that my mother had put up new curtains. It was great to see everyone again and of course there were lots more questions about my work and what I was doing with myself. My mother was especially glad to see that I was happy and making a success of things and I particularly remember Liam having a bit of go and a joke with me for not telling him about my plans to leave. "Oy, you, you bugger, why didn't you tell me you were leaving?" Liam and I had shared a bed and then a bedroom for 20 years, I'm surprised I didn't share my plans with him, now that I think back. We got on well as brothers.

One day Kevin and I walked into Navan and got the train back to Beauparc. He was very keen on trains and although I thought it was a strange thing to do, for no reason, I went along with him of course. We got off at Beauparc station and we decided to call and see our Aunty Alice who was now living close by. Our cousin Phyllis was at home and after a chat and a cup of tea we all decided to go for a walk together. We called for her friend, whose name escapes me but she was a lovely tall girl with very blond hair and we were all in our element as we walked down to Beauparc House. It wasn't long before Kevin was walking ahead of me with just Phyllis, I always think he had a bit of a thing for her so I stayed back and strolled with Phyllis's friend, leaving them to it. We walked up to the boathouse on the south bank of the River Boyne where the small boat used by the local families to cross the river was always tied up during the day. The four of us climbed in and I rowed up the river towards Castlefin and we spent just half an hour idling the time away on a lazy sunny afternoon. It was so peaceful down there on the river, closed off from the whole world by dense woodland on either side. It was such a lovely day out but before long it was time to head back through the woods and back home for dinner. We stopped there a good while, Kevin had a camera and he took many pictures that afternoon, great memories.

Our cousin, John Reilly, drove us into Navan on another day in his car, we went to Smiths pub where we met up with more friends. It was great to be back on old turf, chatting with lads I was familiar with and before long the newspaper was out and everyone started to look at what horses were running that afternoon. John Reilly went to put everyone's bets on at the bookies, I personally didn't back anyone but I remember that Kevin backed the winner, a horse called Icy Calm. "What made you pick that?" I asked "I hope the sea is calmer going home," he replied, as we both recalled the rough Irish Sea crossing we'd experienced the week before. Most nights we'd just ride into Slane and enjoy a few bottles of beer at the hotel bar. It would be pitch black when we'd head off for home and there would often be four or five of us riding out on the Navan Road. Of course, the lights on our bikes were not very powerful, if indeed we had any and occasionally you'd hear the odd profanity in the dark as someone rode into a pothole and came off their bike. One night in particular as we cycled home past the castle, Kevin lagged behind. We'd had a few beers and the ride home was hard on the legs at the best of times but I could hear Kevin puffing and panting behind me as he tackled the long, slow incline up to Cruicetown. All of a sudden he shouted "John, you've gone too far ahead, I can't see where I'm going," and moments later I heard some mild expletives as I heard him stumble into the ditch and fall off his bike like so many before him. Thinking back to that night, still makes me smile but he wasn't used to his surroundings whereas I knew every dip and bump in the road. What struck me most on those rides home during that holiday however was how different it was to living in St. Helens and how easy it is to forget the beauty and peace that comes with the silence of the countryside at night. The absence of streetlights made the stars in the night sky more visible and I was not only struck by how many there were but that I had perhaps taken all this for granted before my move to England. I enjoyed taking Kevin to all the usual places of interest and took pride in showing him my old stomping ground and introducing him to all my old friends. He did enjoy that holiday and we often reminisced about those happy days in fact Kevin accompanied me on each visit home after that until I started to take Rita there several years later.

I always valued my friendship with Kevin and we became closer still after Rita introduced him to her friend Margaret Nulty who he struck up a relationship with. As a foursome we socialised together and holidayed together many, many times, he became my best friend and in our dotage we would still visit The Stanley in Gillers Green Lane, which strangely was one of the first pubs we visited together back in 1949. We would meet up at 9pm every Tuesday and every Thursday right up until he got ill in 2008 and whilst enjoying a couple of pints each we'd chat about good times and bad, friends and family and any topical issue we could think of. Happy days indeed.

Rita and I never discussed getting married or made long-term plans but after we had been together for 12 months I asked her to come back to Ireland with me so that she could meet my family. It was 1951 and we booked an overnight ferry crossing from Liverpool to Dublin and luckily it was a very smooth crossing. She was accustomed to sailing as she'd holidayed in the Isle of Man with her family several times so she was familiar with the port, the ferries and of course, the sail didn't bother her at all. After docking at Dublin, we made our way to the bus station and got the next bus to Navan without any to-do but how we got from Navan to

Stackallan, I really can't remember. I can only imagine that someone picked us up.

Rita was allocated one of the single beds in the big bedroom that the girls used when they were home and once again, my mother had put up fresh new curtains and made the room especially pretty for her. Betty was married and still living at Stackallan Lodge so it was just Delia and Maureen that she shared with and I slept where I used to sleep with the lads.

My parents never asked too many questions, about me, my work or Rita, we all just chatted away naturally and everyone got on

very well. Deep down I knew they thought I was serious about her, why else would I have taken her home. My dad was always a very quiet man but to reassure him, I told him that I was working in a furniture factory, equivalent to the one in Navan, and I could tell he was satisfied with what I was earning and everything I was doing. He would say very little, he really was a very quiet man but he would nod his head as we all talked and that was a sure sign he was

1951 - My parents and Seamus with Rita outside our home

happy enough. I knew that he approved of what I was doing and that he was pleased for me that things were going well because years later, when

Seamus was looking for

Enjoying one of our many picnics on Rita's first trip home

141

work my father said to him "Why don't you go over to the other side, to the other fella, he's done very well for himself."

During that first holiday to Ireland together, I remember thinking that Rita seemed very comfortable and friendly with everyone and the success of that first meeting made me feel more relaxed about our relationship. Knowing that my family accepted and approved of her and that she accepted and approved of my family made me feel very satisfied. We had a whale of a time during that week and I have many fond memories of our first time 'home' together. Someone found us a couple of old bikes and we rode everywhere, into Slane, passed the sawmills where I used to work, Slane castle and finally through the village up to the ruins on the top of the Hill of Slane. It was a lovely day and a strenuous ride so we ended up pushing the bikes to the top of Slane Hill, where we stopped and rested. I pointed out this and that along the way, The Hotel, The Church and we even stopped so that I could show her how we used the water pumps to get water we needed, which of course proved to be a novelty to her.

We went into Navan, and took the bus out to the beach at Bettystown, I took her into Drogheda to show her the head of Blessed Oliver Plunkett at St Peter's Church and out to see the Celtic crosses at Monasterboice. We planned our days carefully to make the most of our holiday and we took picnics with us wherever we went. In the evening, we went to the bar in The Conyngham Arms Hotel in Slane and any dances at Maloney's and I was pleased to introduce her to some of my friends. In particular, I remember going to the village celebrations on 15th August, the day I now know as the Feast of the Assumption, but back then we all referred to it as St. Bridget's day which remained a mystery to me for some time, as St. Bridget's day was actually on 9th February! I later learned that local legend referred to a young child's health improving after St. Bridget appeared to her in the woods, Slane's very own miracle! As a consequence there was a Holy Well deep in the woods and grounds of Slane Castle, were people would walk to collect the water that was subsequently able to heal all ailments. By all accounts, the water was said to dry up again after the week of celebrations and only come back on the following 15th August. I'm not sure many really believed this but many went along with it.

Regardless of the folklore and stories that surrounded the Holy Well, Slane came alive on 15th August. No-one worked that day but everyone would get up early and go to 8am Mass and once the prayers and blessings were over, the festivities started. Everyone in the village had been getting ready for a number of weeks and there was always talk of the upcoming holiday. Who should we meet? When? Where? What time? It was always great fun and the build up to the big day was often as exciting as the day itself. It was quite a spectacle to see my home town come to life like that and I always enjoyed the revelries around that time. Numerous stalls set up along the road and the year Rita first came I was happy just walking amongst them, watching all and sundry joining in with the games on offer. The village was heaving and the pubs were always jam packed as people travelled into the town from all over the County. It was predominantly men that filled the pubs back then but the year I first took Rita was also the only year I ever saw my mother in a pub. She was with Mrs. McGrath from The Post Office, the lady who used to take charge of the amateur dramatics. I was actually quite surprised to see my mother holding a glass of wine as I don't think I had ever seen her drink alcohol before, but nevertheless I walked over to say hello and introduce Rita to Mrs. McGrath. I remember to this day, how excited Mrs. McGrath was to see me and she of course made a huge fuss of Rita. I liked that.

I think Rita enjoyed the music most of all and she often said through later years that it was that first 'carnival' she went to in Slane that gave her love of Irish Music. She was a great piano player and she had good rhythm, which also made her a fabulous little dancer and I can still visualise her where we stopped to have some tea and cake with her feet and hands tapping away to the background music made by a small group of locals playing tin whistles, accordions and of course the bodhran. I bumped in to many familiar faces, several old school friends and work colleagues and it seemed like an endless day of introductions for Rita. I remember being as proud as punch. It was a long and very enjoyable day and a day neither of us ever forgot and even the long walk back home in the pitch black didn't appear as tedious as usual as we caught up with other stragglers laughing and chatting along the way.

The pilgrimage up to the Holy Well, the day's festivities and of course the aftermath was always well talked about. I didn't always walk up to the well itself, I was able to walk freely around the grounds of the estate when the family were away but for many, my mother included, it was especially nice to venture into territory the majority were not normally allowed to visit. The excitement of being allowed through the Gothic Gate by Slane Bridge seemed to make the day more special for many and when I was a working boy up at the sawmills I remember John Heavy, Paddy Lanney and the Vesey brothers putting all their energy into preparing those parts of the grounds in readiness. Lady Conynham wanted the grounds to look nice for her visitors.

Closer to home however and much more accessible to me was the water from St. Patrick's Well and I can't count the number of times that I visited there to collect water for my mother. It was lovely and clean and great to taste and even on my trips home to Ireland over the years I would make my way down to it, either on my own or with my little family. I would busy myself clearing away any debris to keep the waters clear but over the years as I visited less and less, the task got harder and harder. I'm sure St. Patrick's

Well is still there but it won't really be relevant to anyone now, it's sad to think that but it gave me hours of fun over the years.

My brother Seamus thought Rita was absolutely wonderful and was always around her skirts. They developed a great relationship, as she did with all my brothers and sisters, my parents too but she and Delia, who visited us in England annually were particularly close. They would gossip, share stories and shop to their hearts content when they were together, they were great friends indeed. Rita's love of Ireland was recognized by many and I was always so proud of her for embracing my family and my home so warmly. She undoubtedly enjoyed her first holiday with my family, and her first impressions were reassuringly good. I think she initially thought we were wealthy too as she noticed my father had a large amount of money in his wallet. When we were chatting on the ferry home she asked me about it and I was quick to explain that we weren't wealthy at all, just hard-working and that my father had recently sold a cow, which accounted for the money. This seemed to amuse her for some reason. She also was surprised at how my father spoke to my mother, "Mammy, clean my shoes, Mammy make some tea, Mammy do this, Mammy do that ..." It's the way we were, the way we lived, it was the way it was - all perfectly natural for us but it was different enough for Rita to make her remark.

Visiting St. Patrick's Well, with Rita in 1950, Martin and Amanda in 1963. Damian joins us in 1970 along with my cousin Kevin Riley's daughter Shelagh.

10
No Going Back

I don't remember asking Rita to marry me but I think it was when we were cuddling one evening in the 'Picture House'. I doubt she'd know herself if she was here to ask, we talked about our future together often and it was a foregone conclusion that we would get engaged soon. It was 1952, when I bought her engagement ring and it was whilst we were on another holiday In Ireland. We bought it from the 'best shop in Dublin' and she picked it herself. I would never have dreamt of picking one out on my own, I wanted her to have her own choice and she made a good choice, three diamonds set in white gold. I was earning £8/12/- a week at the time and I paid £26 for it. After the assistant but it in a box, I slipped it in to my pocket for an appropriate time but on leaving the shop we went to the pictures and she couldn't rest, she kept nudging me for the ring, "Where is it?, Where is it?, John, John, where is it?" she kept whispering and so I gave in and gave her the ring there and then. I hadn't really made my mind up when to give it to her or whether to propose more formally, but she didn't want to wait, she always was very impatient.

Rita took me to Jameson and Jones, a tailor's shop at the bottom of Moss Street in Liverpool and I paid £19/19/- to have a suit made for my wedding. It was 1st November 1952. I generally wore a sports jacket and a pair of flannels as I loved that look for going out at night, I didn't wear a suit very much but I wanted her to be proud of me so went along with it. There was also a good tailor's shop in Prescot Town Centre next to Rays Bakery called Roberts and Bromley and a couple of years later, I had a jacket and flannels made there too. I remember looking at several lengths of cloth with Rita and eventually picked out a grey material. They cost me

£16/16/- in 1954 which today would be about £140. Not bad for a lad from the banks of the Boyne.

Our first little holiday together, away from Ireland was to Torquay in 1952 and we went with my cousin Kevin and his girlfriend Margaret Nulty. We travelled by train which was quite an adventure for me in itself and we arrived much later than anticipated after the train broke down in a tunnel along the way. What a disastrous start, all the lights went out, it went pitch black and because it was so late it went very cold, so we huddled together to keep warm and listened to everyone complaining. It was some time before we got going again and it was the middle of the night before we arrived at our hotel. The owner was not happy with us at all and didn't seem interested in our explanation for being so late. We stayed in a place called Meadfoot Beach. None of us had been there before and we were all just tagged along after Kevin who held the maps after organising the whole trip. Years later he told me that he only chose that location so that he could enjoy a long train ride!

Relaxing on the beach (in full jacket, shirt and tie!)

Outside our hotel

It must have been in the summer months as everywhere was busy and there were plenty of guests staying in the hotel, but nevertheless it didn't stop the proprietor keeping a close eye on us, at least that's what we thought! Each evening at bed time he would take himself off from his bar duties and go and sit on the small landing quite close to our bedrooms. I didn't notice at first but Kevin cottoned onto it and said to me quietly one evening "that fella is watching us like a hawk, he wants to make sure that we don't go in with the girls." It wasn't ever our intention and whereas many would have taken the opportunity, we were honourable young men. His antics amused us all greatly, especially as he would pretend to read the newspaper and we often considered how long he would sit there each evening before being satisfied with our behaviour. Each morning, we'd get up and shave, get ready and knock on the girls' door to say we were going down to breakfast and they would join us soon after. Most days we would walk down to the beach and sit on deck chairs in the day chatting and relaxing, enjoying ice creams and occasionally fish and chips. We spent a lot of time on the beach before heading back to the hotel to freshen up for dinner and then into the hotel bar for a few drinks. We took a day trip out to Buckfast Abbey and to the edge of Dartmoor where we had time to walk around the hills on our own for a long while. It was very barren, nice country to walk in but a very different landscape to what I was used to and there were the ponies of course. It was a new experience for me and I loved it all. It was a typical English seaside holiday, the first of many enjoyable holidays we had together as couples and as great friends.

Rita busied herself with wedding plans and we chose to get married, exactly three years after we first met, on 14th February 1953 at Our Lady's and St. Joseph's RC Church in Prescot - true Valentines indeed. Our Lady's church meant a lot to Rita and her family so it was the obvious choice for us. My parents couldn't come to the wedding but my father's brother Harry and his family, who all lived in St. Helens, represented my family and my sisters, Delia and Maureen, travelled across for the celebrations. Delia was 'chief' bridesmaid, so the Reillys played a substantial part on the day and we were delighted to receive a telegram from home wishing us well. We had an afternoon celebration upstairs at The Hope and Anchor Public House on Prescot High Street and then we honeymooned in Ireland, where else! We treated ourselves to a cabin on the ferry whilst it was a special occasion and laughed when we found there were bunk beds in there. Oh well.

Left to Right - Uncle Harry, Delia, Maureen, Me, Rita, Frances Moran (mother-in-law), Kevin Riley (Best Man), Tom Moran (father-in-law). Young bridesmaid on left is Susan Hampson (niece) and Barbara Moran (niece) on right

Rita's family had made me feel very welcome from the beginning. Her sister Mary was married to Jimmy Hampson and they had three young daughters, Susan, Janet and Kathryn and her brother Vincent and his wife Sybil had three children at the time too, Barbara, Geoffrey and Phillip. Rita's parent's, Tom and Frances Moran well and truly adopted me and on the whole I couldn't have hoped for a better extended family. Tom even lent us £500 so we could buy our first house, which was a little two up two down in Evans Street, Prescot - number 21. A butcher by trade, he was always very kind to me and I was only content to borrow the money on the proviso that we had a proper repayment plan in place. Tom took charge and each week he would mark off in a little book the £1/9/- we paid back regularly.

It was only a small house and we didn't have a lot but we were very happy in those first years. The lads in Freeman's factory had made us a couple of chairs as our wedding present and I had picked out a dining table that I fancied which I was allowed to buy at cost price. We did not have a television, just a Redifusion wireless box, which we rented for 2/6- every fortnight but we considered ourselves to be very lucky. We read the local newspapers and listened to news programs but in those early days we enjoyed a simple life, walking and chatting to our neighbours who we got on very well with. We were very settled there. I remained happy at Freeman's furniture factory and Rita was in her element teaching English and Music at St. Dominic's in Huyton so in the evening she would generally be preparing lessons and doing school work. She was such a hard worker and always dedicated to her profession and as a consequence I became a 'modern man' and helped around the home. I didn't miss Ireland as much as I thought but I sense that was because I was fully occupied and exceptionally happy. I did often wonder about friends from home and what they were doing. I knew Aidan Meade had become the doctor he had always dreamed of becoming and I knew that my good friend Liam Feeley had joined the airforce. My mother wrote to me often and I would always welcome her letters which kept me informed of local news and gossip from home and of course 17th March did not pass by without the obligatory salute to St. Patrick.

The Blessing of God and St. Patrick be with you

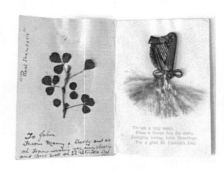

Examples of the small tokens I would receive from my mother on St. Patrick's Day

Liam Feeley was a couple of months older than me, he was born on 29th June 1927 and he left home before me. I heard he joined the airforce by travelling to Drogheda and then on to Belfast, Northern Ireland where he did a couple of weeks training. By all accounts he was in the airforce for 25 years and he stayed in England all that time. Years later after I'd been living in England for 30 years or so, I thought I recognised him in a store and approached him. I couldn't believe the coincidence and soon discovered that he was living in Crosby, a mere 15 miles away from each other and we didn't even know it. I used to see him quite regularly after that for a short while but with the passage of time, we had different interests and our friendship petered out. Last I heard he was in Aintree Hospital and was suffering from Alzheimers Disease and despite Amanda's efforts to organise a reunion, his wife was reluctant due to his condition so I let things be.

Epilogue

Remarkably, at the point of my father's death in May 2016, we had reached a natural point in his storytelling where his book might end. He had arrived in England and he had met my mother, his life ahead was a new chapter. He felt that few would be interested in his English memories, of which we documented many, as this life was much more traditional or 'normal' as he put it. I disagreed but to be respectful to his wishes, this book is mainly about Ireland and his life there, that's the way he wanted it.

He led a good and honourable life. He did as his father asked of him on the night he sailed to England, he 'kept his religion' and remained a devout and popular figure in the Catholic community of Prescot and he of course stayed clear of 'funny women', enjoying 54 happy years of marriage to my mother. He continued to work at Freeman's Furniture Factory until 1955 when he spotted an advert in the local paper seeking Insurance Agents for The Prudential Assurance Company. My mother felt his six years of very basic education may not be enough to secure the position he fancied but supported his ambition and worked at home in the evenings preparing him for a formal interview. Strangely, this took place in their home in Evans Street and was conducted by Mr. Bearpark, the Prudential's North West Area Manager who welcomed his application, however, because his place of birth was listed as Ireland and because the nature of the job was sales, Mr. Bearpark was in reality sent to determine whether his accent was understandable and not too pronounced to detract from the work. He recognised my father's warm and sincere nature immediately, that he was a confident young man who possessed a natural 'gift of the gab' and as a consequence, Mr. Bearpark announced there and then that he thought he would be ideally suited to the role. Before long, he had tendered his resignation and ended his career as a wood machinist and embarked on his long and fruitful career as 'The Man from the PRU'. He remained loyal to the company until his retirement in 1986 and was recognised for his achievements on several occasions. He had numerous invitations to the 'Star Dinner' in glitzy London hotels in acknowledgement of his excellent work and distinction, a merited honour that he was particularly proud of.

THE PRUDENTIAL ASSURANCE COMPANY LIMITED.
(INCORPORATED IN ENGLAND)

HOLBORN BARS, LONDON, E.C.1.

OUR REF. A/G

YOUR REF.

11th March, 1963.

Mr. J.P. Reilly,
District Agent,
St.Helens,
G.37-1569.

re:- General Manager's Celebration
Dinner, 1963.

Dear Sir,

I feel sure you will be gratified to learn that your name is included in the list of those representatives whose services during 1962 are deemed to have been of exceptional merit, and I have much pleasure, therefore, in sending you an official invitation to the General Manager's Celebration Dinner to be held on the 8th May, 1963.

It would be a
as earl

J.P.REILLY
St. Helens

THE PRUDENTIAL ASSURANCE CO. LTD

This Certificate is awarded to

Mr J.P.Reilly

in recognition of specially meritorious service
to the Company during the year 1962

May 8th 1963

General Manager

155

In 1957, life changed for the better following the arrival of my sister Paula. My father explained that every morning, Mum would get her ready and dress her in some of the nicest baby clothes that he had ever seen, she would put her in her Silver Cross pram and after she left to catch the bus to work, he would take her in the pram, through Knowsley Park Lane and

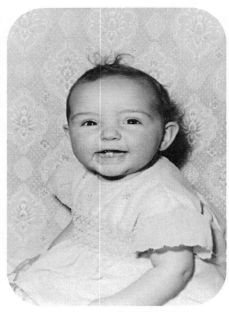

Paula Mary Reilly 1957-1958

down to my grandparents' house at 50 South Avenue, Prescot. My father's new job meant that he worked more in the evening selling insurance when people were more likely to be at home and as a consequence, he enjoyed a lot of flexibility during the day. My grandmother or 'Nanna' as we all referred to her as, looked after Paula during the day until such time as my father was free to walk back and collect her in time for Mum finishing work.

During the summer of 1957, they all travelled home to Ireland to introduce Paula to the rest of the family and everyone was overjoyed to welcome the latest addition to the Reilly clan. My father always maintained that he wasn't a particularly 'hands-on' father and that my mum took complete charge of all parental duties, so much so that my Nanna apparently said to her on one occasion, "Rita, you're making too much fuss of that baby, be careful, sometimes they are only lent." By all accounts, my mother thought this was a particularly cruel thing for her own mother to say and was hurt by the remark, but my father felt that she was just guarding my mum against becoming too attached to her child in such a fragile world and as history unfolded, those words resonated throughout their lives.

Paula died in February 1958 when only 12 months old and I know this loss hit both my parents exceptionally hard. She was a healthy child that suddenly became very ill and for six weeks they watched her change. The local GP visited the house each week but insisted that my mum was being an anxious, first time mother, he called her neurotic and continued to maintain that there wasn't anything seriously wrong with Paula. Being from the generation that didn't question professionals, my parents accepted the doctor's word but after a particularly bad 'fit' one evening the doctor finally called for an ambulance which immediately took them all to Whiston Hospital. Staff there initially criticised my parents for not bringing Paula to them sooner until they explained that they had called the doctor out to see her in their home every week for the last six weeks! Dad recalled the silence and stared at stunned faces as they explained the gravity of her illness. She remained in hospital and arrangements were made for Fr. Horan to confirm and anoint her before they were asked to leave. Having left the house in such a hurry, they had little money on them, no coats and only slippers on their feet and by the time they had walked the mile home it was midnight and they were cold and frightened. In describing this awful wet and windy night that neither of them ever forgot, my father's most vivid memory was of my mum stood in the rain outside the main entrance to Whiston hospital, looking lost and terrified, as she broke her heart crying but above anything else, he recalled how totally helpless and ill equipped he felt, he wondered how on earth he was ever going to help her. They clearly did not want to leave Paula but there were no facilities for them to stay, it wasn't acceptable back then which to me now seems so cruel and left with

157

no choice they reluctantly went home. Paula's health deteriorated during the night and a telegram was sent out to them to visit immediately but by the time they reached the ward, Paula had already died. My father remembers that they were taken aside and treated very sympathetically but he remembers little of what was said. The cause of death was tubercular meningitis, she had been ill for six weeks. How cruel this all seems and how different it would be today and despite my father being a very forgiving man, he never, ever spoke highly of the doctor that failed to recognise the severity of her illness or do anything to help them. He described Paula's loss as an overwhelming and unbearable sadness, "We cried and cried and cried for a long time after that." In his own final weeks, when he would often say his prayers aloud I was surprised that he never mentioned her name in the long list of people he prayed for and when I asked why, he replied in such a gentle manner, "I don't have to pray for Paula, there's no need - she's already an Angel." I loved him dearly for the simplicity of that statement and I wish I had the same level of surety and the strength of his belief.

After Paula's death in 1958, they moved house for a fresh start and to be a little closer to my grandparents, it was the same year, my father bought his first car. With increased wages from The Prudential and my mother's good teacher's salary, they took advantage of attractive interest rates offered to Prudential employees. The interest rate at the time was only 2.5% which he described as a gift. To enable him to drive in England, my father simply wrote to his brother-in-law, Tom Gray, in Beauparc and asked him for an Irish Driving Licence Application Form, filling it in as though he still lived in Cruicetown. He then sent it back to Tom who took the forms to the offices in Navan where a licence was immediately despatched. It seems that the documented history of driving agricultural machinery on many different farms in Ireland was all that was needed to demonstrate his ability, and he drove without a glitch on the UK roads for over 50 years without ever having to take a driving test!

The house my parents bought in Wood Lane, Prescot needed quite a bit of work doing to it and so there was a lot of decorating in the early days which they embraced as a welcome distraction from their recent tragedy. By all accounts, my Aunty Mary, my mother's sister helped out a lot and my father's cousin Kevin came and helped build a garage for the new car in the back garden. Mrs. Evans, the old lady that lived opposite them on Preston Avenue bought them some lovely etched glass lampshades when they moved in, which they thought were very classy and despite the passage of time, they are as good now as the day they were given to my father. They have pride of place in my own home now, antiques perhaps! My father enjoyed doing the garden and the flower beds, it wasn't a big garden and he reckoned it only took him an hour or so to tidy up, but it was pleasurable enough and he tried to keep it nice.

Lillian Wales lived next door and had done from a young age. Lilian had been in the Ladies Army and never married and constantly often looked to my father when she needed help. She would often bang on the adjoining wall and shout "John, John, are you there?" And of course my father would run around to see how he could help. I remember her being sad when we left the house in 1971.

In between times, the pain from Paula's early death subsided a little and life for my parents resumed to some sort of normality. My brother Martin was born in 1959 and I followed in 1960 before Damian arrived as a late addition in 1966. Although well and truly enveloped within the bosom of my mother's parents, whom we lovingly called Nanna and Grandpa, my father ensured his own family remained pivotal in our lives too. Most summers were

159

spent holidaying in and around Slane, my Aunty Delia, who had never married, visited for two weeks every year and there was also the occasional visit from my Grandpa and Granny Reilly.

A bad experience in 1969 however whilst travelling through Belfast in the north of Ireland curtailed our travels 'home' for a while. As per usual we drove to Stranraer in Scotland to get the shorter two and a half hours crossing over to Larne in Northern Ireland, instead of the eight-hour crossing from Liverpool. We followed the usual route south through Belfast City Centre, through Newry, across the border, through Dundalk and onto Slane, a trip we had taken many times without incident. In 1969 however, Belfast was noticeably chaotic as there was a protest of some description and a very angry crowd. Before long our car and caravan became the focus of their disgruntlement for a while and as well as banging on the car with their fists, they jeered at us chanting 'Brits out. Brits out!' I was only nine years old and I remember being really frightened and of course looking back now it was clear we drove directly through a war zone during what is now referred to as 'The Troubles'. I imagine they targeted us because of the English number plates and of course they couldn't have realised the car was being driven by one of their own. We ended up getting a police escort out of the city but the experience shook us all and we didn't go back to Ireland for a while after that, in fact I think thereafter we always took the safer route from Liverpool to Dún Laoghaire, despite the long and often unpleasant Irish Sea crossing.

My father flew to Ireland for his father's funeral in 1971. I was close by when the telephone call came through to say that Grandpa Reilly was gravely ill and I witnessed Dad's sadness on taking that news. I remember watching my father leave for the airport in his dark suit almost immediately after. He made his way directly to Navan hospital from Dublin airport and thankfully had time with his father before he died. He never really said much more

160

about that time other than that he was able to sit by his father's side and ponder about all the happy times that he had spent with him. He was always grateful for that.

By this time we had moved to Albany Avenue in Eccleston Park, Prescot and although we weren't visiting Ireland as regularly anymore, my father's sister Delia was still holidaying with us annually. I would willingly surrender my bedroom for two weeks every year and in turn she would teach me all manner of things, how to cook, bake, make my own sauces, how to fillet fish, how to make toys, dresses, crochet and knit and of course her love of tennis and Wimbledon was legendary. When I was off school in the summer holidays, tennis on the TV in the afternoon with tea, strawberries and cream, became our passion. Without doubt, our ties to Cruicetown, Slane and Ireland remained as strong as ever and 1978 was a holiday there that I will always cherish. With 'The Troubles' losing momentum we went back 'home' on our first family

holiday for some time, sadly it was also our last holiday to Ireland as a complete family, for in 1980 life dealt my parents another cruel blow when my older brother Martin was tragically killed in a car accident on 14th August while on holiday in America. He was a 21 year old law student and had

Martin Gerard Reilly 1959-1980

embarked on a working holiday before starting back in his final year at university. It was an absolute tragedy, he was a young, charismatic and energetic individual, the life and soul wherever he went and his loss simply devastated us all. I don't think I can begin

161

to explain how we all felt at that time I know I was numb for a long time but for this to happen to my parents twice, it's difficult to understand how they coped. Not only did my parents have to deal with their own grief but they had to try and make sense of what happened whilst continuing to support Damian and I struggle with our brother's unexpected and untimely death. During conversations with the American authorities my parents did not receive any respect, support or sympathy and I recall that my mum was offended on numerous occasions and specifically by the directness and tactlessness of staff in the Coroner's office. With the help of family and friends from within the Church, Martin's body eventually arrived home on 18th August and that day became the first day of a new life for us all. A life less vibrant, a life less joyful and a life with more tears. I was 20 and my younger brother Damian was only 14 when the accident happened, I just remember that it was a sad, sad summer. On reflection, it hit my father hardest and he became quite unwell, my mother was the strength behind us all and she worked hard keeping her small grieving family together. For the very first time, all my father's siblings travelled together and came to England for their nephew's funeral, a show of solidarity in adversity and a demonstration of a close knit and loving family, despite the miles that separated them. Amongst the sadness, I do remember there being moments of laughter when we were all together but above all, I do know that it helped my father deal with the loss of his eldest son and his second child, they became his crutch and he lent on them when he needed them most of all.

We remained a happy family unit but we all knew there was a vital element missing. My father busied himself in and around his garden, he had a small woodwork shed where he seemed happiest and he created and executed his own little projects. He built his first ever greenhouse himself and eventually picked up a saw bench and a lathe which for safety, were all kept under lock and key. He progressed to making spindles and other decorative objects but his pride and joy had to be the solid wood gates which sectioned off the back of the family home. I drive past the old house every now and then and feel a sense of pride when I see that they are still there, I also know that his initials are carved into the back of them and that makes me smile too. Good old JPR!

Left to Right - Maureen, Betty, Delia (top)
Seamus, Patsy, Liam and John (bottom)

He had quite a substantial plot of land at the back of the house which was divided into two sections by his own hand made trellis. The front part was lawn with shrubs and flowers which my mother tended to, whilst the lower part was sectioned off for all manner of fruit and vegetables. He mainly grew potatoes, onions, leeks, cabbages as well as tomatoes, cucumbers, peppers and lettuce and all from seed. He tried his hand at marrow, herbs, strawberries and often several different varieties at once, yet to his dismay he never managed to grow particularly good carrots, something that always bewildered him. He would chat to his brother Patsy, who was also a keen gardener, for hours on end about what they were growing and their luck that year with produce. There were two old apples trees in the garden that produced an abundance of apples every year but Dad also planted a couple of damson trees and several gooseberry bushes just like in the kitchen garden at Castlefin and around the house at Cruicetown. The damson trees mainly reminded him of his time at Castlefin where his mother would make jars and jars of both damson and gooseberry jam for all and sundry. Like in Ireland, the fruit grew in abundance and like in Ireland, after taking what we needed for ourselves he would distribute the remainder of what he grew to friends, family and even clients and it would not be usual to see visitors leave our home with bags brimming with fruit and vegetables. He loved his plot and I loved to watch him tilling, sowing and harvesting. I was always happy to lend a hand and get involved every now and then. For my father though, it was his passion and the garden was where he would take himself off to, to escape from his troubles, from pressures of work and from mundane routines. In 1981 as I watched him working from my bedroom window for several hours, I penned these few words. He would work, he would sit and rest and I watched him ponder. He would work some more, rest some more and ponder some more...I could see how happy he was and I loved him for that.

My father in his cherished garden

He Digs On

He stands surveying what lies in front of him,

He begins his mammoth task and stabs the rich earth.

Age creeping upon him, he hesitates and ponders, raising his

face to the sky.

The sky clouds over and the storm breaks but he ploughs on,

his task needs to be done.

Figures and papers are forgotten, his mind is tranquil and

content, full of what he loves –

It is his world, it belongs to him and he to it.

The smile on his wrinkled face is enough to say he is happy,

I watch him from afar and imagine boyhood days tingling in his

mind,

When life was the life he loved, the fields, the country smells,

the green land, his green land, his green country and his home.

Nothing is ever forgotten, he continues to reflect on those happy

days of youth,

but time will wait for no man, the rain pours and his smile fades,

He comes back to today but longs for tomorrow.

He digs on.

I supported my father and was by his side when my own mother
died in October 2007, when his brother Liam died in 2008, his dear
friend and cousin Kevin in 2009 and his sister Maureen several years

later. As when Martin died, throughout all these life events, my father turned to his faith, he sought solace in the arms of the Church and got his strength from his friends within Portico Parish, the Church he first visited back in 1949.

After my mother died I took him home to Ireland several times but that first holiday without her in April 2008 was perhaps the most difficult. When I look back at photographs of that time he just looks lost and in some photographs I've even unwittingly managed to capture his sadness, after all it was his first journey home without my mum by his side since 1951. At his request, we followed the same routine and visited the same familiar places but this time his energy went into showing his grand-daughter Jennifer what he had showed my brothers and I years before. This time I stood by and watched him draw water from the pump outside his old school house for her, watched him at Rushwee Chapel tell her the story of his rolling penny, watched as we stood by the old ruined Woollen Mill by Stackallan Bridge as he told her of his childhood playground. Like me, Jennifer has been down to Loc Chaisléan na Finne, like me she has and always will have a sense of 'belonging' to the wonderful and lush Boyne Valley, but how did an old man manage to instil these feelings and this passion in us from so far away? The answer is that he simply loved the place where he grew up, he was in awe of both his parents for what they had achieved from very little and he was exceptionally proud of his humble beginnings. He spoke passionately about his family and his life back then and he made sure that despite the miles, we all remained closely entwined.

On 22nd May 2016 my father succumbed to his illness and died at home as he wished, with my brother and I at his side and with his rosary beads in his hands. He was a good man and he led a good life. He had a charming naivety and innocence about him, his generosity was boundless and he was such a selfless man, who went through his whole life putting others first. He was a gentle soul, chivalrous and the phrase I hear most of all when he is spoken of - he was always a 'true gentleman'. He was placid, mild mannered and content, he never raised his voice and he had a calming and soothing presence - always. He taught me patience, serenity and understanding, particularly in his latter years and I learned from him every day. Not only did he teach me how to behave, he shared practical advice too. He taught me how to fish, how to use a drill, how to wallpaper, how to get the best out of my garden and would often say I was better at DIY than either of his two sons. Considerably less practical but nevertheless memorable, he also taught me how to kill and cook fresh eels, how to pluck and clean pheasants and how to make and set a snare should I need to catch the rabbits that were beginning to invade my garden. Thank goodness he didn't realise my neighbours kept chickens!!

He worked hard, was a devoted husband, and showed me what a good and proper marriage should look like, how to always be respectful and how to be there for each other, in the best of times and in the worst of times. He set a fine example to both my brother and I, instilled values that we are proud to pass onto our own children and I feel honoured that he belonged to me!

I am delighted to share his memories and the valuable insight he has provided into the rural community that influenced him so strongly and made him the man he became. He was my father, my teacher and my friend and although I will miss every ounce of his being, I know his memory will now live on. What a remarkable achievement for a boy from the 'riverside' with just six years of schooling - how proud am I!

Standing on the ramparts outside the ruins of Chaisléan na Finne in 2013. Left to Right - My sister-in-law Susan, my niece Martha, my daughter Jennifer, me with my nephew Edward (infront), my brother Damian and my husband Geoff. This photo always had pride of place in my father's home.

<u>Annex</u>

A brief family history of The Reilly and Harding families.

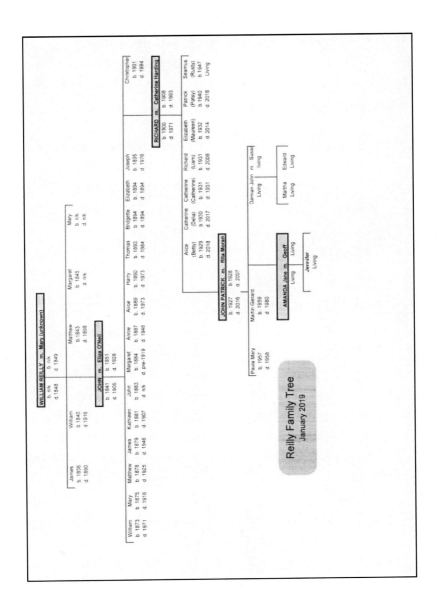

Reilly Family Tree
January 2019

Paternal Great Grandparents of John Patrick Reilly

William Reilly	m.	Mary (Unknown)
b. Unknown		b. Unknown
d. 1848		d. 1849

Children of William and Mary Reilly

1. James Reilly b. 1836. James was the eldest child, as far as I have been able to determine, of my great-grandparents William and Mary Reilly. My father told me stories as a boy of family in faraway places and I learned about his three adventurous uncles James, William and Matthew who had emigrated to America as young men from an early age. In 1993, I travelled to America on holiday with my wife Rita and we visited James' granddaughter Mary Nemec. She shared a lot of information about her grandfather and in particular this photograph, I wonder if he was one of the faces that I used to see in the purple velvet family album many, many years ago? Mary Nemec was able to tell me that James was the eldest of my grandfather's generation and that he travelled to America in 1858 as a young man of 22, the same age as me, when I left home! He travelled and worked in Canada initially before returning to America where he enlisted in the 2nd New York Rifles and fought in The American Civil War under the pseudonym James Foley. To avoid fighting it was quite common for young, wealthy American men to pay others to fight on their

172

behalf so I imagine James Reilly saw an opportunity and took the money for someone. He survived the war and settled in Cleveland Ohio where he married a widow by the name of Mrs. Mary Murray who had five children of her own. He worked on the railways as a brakeman and latterly a yardmaster and settled close to his brothers William and Matthew who also emigrated. Historical records show that he used several spellings of his surname (Reilly, Reiley and Riley) which makes research interesting. He died in 1890 and left a widow and step-children as well as five children of his own, William b.1871, Mary Ellen b.1873, Katherine b.1876, Agnes Mae b.1880 and Arthur James b.1882. Mary Reilly Nemec is Arthur's youngest child. I have photographs, newspaper articles and historical records of James' life and time in the war, which demonstrate the full and interesting life he had and thanks to Mary I have been able to draft quite a compressive family tree. My daughter Amanda and Mary's daughter Carolyn are friends on social media.

2. **William Reilly b. 1840** As far as I am aware, William is the second child of William and Mary Reilly. From his photograph I don't doubt that he is an uncle as in my eyes, he bears a strong resemblance to my own father, my Uncle Harry and even myself as I progressed in years. His death certificate states that he was Captain William James Reilly and born in Ireland in 1841, however the 1900 US census states he was born in April 1840 and that he emigrated to America in 1850. This would place his

emigration immediately after the deaths of his parents and as a young boy of ten, which I'm not sure is too realistic and certainly doesn't fit with any family information. Other documentation shows later emigration dates of 1853 and 1863 but as many forms were often filled in by other family members, there is no guarantee that any of them are correct. William married Carrie De Etta Rose on 2.9.1874 and they had five children together, William, Caroline, Fred, Lillian Belle and John Rose Reilly. Carrie however divorced William and moved to California with some of her children, she marries an Edward Quiggin in 1895 and John Quarmby in 1904. William however stays in Cleveland Ohio and died on 21.3.1916 in the home of his daughter Caroline. Ancestors in this branch of the family appear to have had considerable wealth and travelled extensively but sadly, William's son John Rose Reilly committed suicide in 1931 'after suffering financial losses and becoming despondent'. When the U.S. stock market crashed in 1929, the consequences rippled across the country, I suspect John Rose Reilly may have been a casualty of that. How tragic and how desperate must a young man be to pull a gun on himself. John Rose Reilly left behind a widow and a son, who was only 11 years old at the time. He however grew up to be a movie star and appeared in films such as '30 Seconds Over Tokyo' with Spencer Tracy and Ernie Pyle's 'Story of G. I. Joe'. A young man with a Hollywood smile - a far cry from his grandfather's upbringing in the midst of The Irish Famine. Only recently have we established closer links with William's descendants, Lorraine Thomas and Alexander Djordevich, again through social media and Amanda regularly shares family research material with each of them.

3. **John Reilly b.1841** was my grandfather but there is an anomaly with his date of birth. The Irish Census of 1901 records his age as 60, hence 1841 but his death certificate of 1905 states that he was 77 years old when he died on 28.1.1905. This would place his date of birth as 1828 and much older than his siblings. It would also make him nearly 30 years older than his wife and 73 when he fathered his youngest child! The 'informant' on the death certificate was John's son Harry, who would have been only 15 at the time and so I am inclined to accept the census data as being more accurate. My grandfather John married Elizabeth O'Neil, he was the Lock Keeper at Castle Fin Lock and he allegedly fathered 22 children! I know very little else about my grandfather, I know he was a lock keeper, I know he applied for a dog licence every year for his red terrier and I know he kept goats! Amanda found all this out on her computer and I think the extent of the information that is available is truly amazing. I also know that in 1874, when my grandfather was 33 and living in Castlefin Lock, his neighbour Luke Maguire, fellow lock keeper and possibly friend, shot and killed his son after a brawl. Two years previously, as outlined in The Irish Times newspaper article below, Luke's wife had drowned in the River Boyne in tragic circumstances.

FORESTER'S[3] FETES – SLANE CASTLE

The large body of Foresters who, accompanied by their wives and children, proceeded on Monday morning from the Amiens-street Terminus to enjoy a Whit Monday holiday on the northern banks of the Boyne,

---

[3] *The Irish National Foresters' Benefit Society was an Irish friendly society. It supported Irish nationalism and its constitution called for "government for Ireland by the Irish people in accordance with Irish ideas and Irish aspirations".*

within the magnificent demesne of the Most Noble the Marquis of Conyngham, participated in one of the most agreeable excursions that could take place in any province of Ireland. A fatal accident, however occurred, which marred to no small extent the pleasure of the excursionists, although they were in no way responsible for it, but the accident happened within a short distance of that part of the demesne in which the Foresters and their friends were enjoying themselves, and intelligence of it having reached the pleasure-seekers, it was heard with no small regret. A woman named Maguire, wife of Luke Maguire, a lock-keeper, residing in the immediate locality, was about crossing from the southern bank of the river to the opposite side, probably intending to witness the sports of the day, but before she had quite taken her seat in the small boat, she fell back into the water, making however a gallant struggle for her life. She swam some distance, and kept herself well above the water, but it was sad in the last degree that her efforts were unavailing, although there were two young men in the boat who, if they had any smartness whatever, might have saved her. The poor woman was within a comparatively short distance of the southern bank, on which at the time there were but a few people, while on the northern bank there were a good many who could scarcely have anticipated that the two young men who were in the boat were so absolutely helpless as they proved themselves. They rowed about wildly, and when at one time they passed the drowning woman so near almost as to be able to reach her by stretching a hand, they put out the oar, which she was unable to seize, and they made no further effort to save her. They rowed immediately to the landing on the south bank, while the people on the north side were filled with indignation that a gallant life should be lost, and that these that had the means of saving her — the easily managed boat in which the two men were — were so utterly useless in the position in which they were placed. The excuse made for them was that they could not swim, and that they were inexperienced as oarsmen. The body of the poor woman was recovered in about twenty minutes after, and every effort was made to resuscitate life, but without success. Mrs. Maguire leaves a husband and several children to mourn her. She was 45 years of age. With regard to the fetes, the Foresters of Dublin, who number 1,500, were largely represented on Monday morning at the Amiens-st. terminus, from which, accompanied by the banners of their various courts, they proceeded by special trains to Beauparc station. On arriving here, the Foresters, of whom a considerable number were beautifully dressed in the costume of their Order, formed themselves into a procession, headed by the fine band of the 16th Regiment, under the direction of Signor Cecconi, and in this order they marched some miles before reaching the bridge by which The Boyne is crossed, within a short distance of the east gate of Lord Conyngham's magnificent park. The band played a number of exquisite airs along the road and when passing through the miles of avenue which led to the famous Castle of Slane, one section of the excursionists, preferring to take a shorter route, walked, by kind permission of the proprietor, Gustavus Lambert, Esq., through his charming demesne of Beauparc. This route lay mostly

177

along the splendidly wooded banks of The Boyne — forming one of the most delightful walks imaginable. Over and over again the Foresters and their friends expressed their gratitude for the treat afforded them by the Marquis of Conyngham in permitting them to enjoy their fetes within his demesne, and they were not less grateful to Mr. Lambert, who without any formal application to him, threw open his demesne to the excursionists. The Foresters selected a gentle eminence within the demesne of Slane Castle, where, with picturesque effect they planted their banners. Meantime they formed themselves into small picnic parties, and after partaking of the generous viands, with which they had provided themselves, they were again prepared to resume those active pleasures which are the more appreciated when they are accompanied by the sounds of sweet music. The band of the Meath Militia, under the command of Mr. Rance, was present and, alternatively with the band of the 16th Regiment played some choice selections of music. Messers. Gulliver and Harold, negro vocalists and comedians, contributed largely to the entertainment, which at great expense the Foresters had provided for themselves. A very large number of people from Drogheda, Navan, Kells, and the various towns within easy distance from Slane, availed themselves of the opportunity afforded them to enjoy the pleasures of the day with the Foresters. The officers of the Order present were — Mr. Wm. Dowling, D.C.R., Mr. H. Lawless, S.D.C.R., Mr. John D. Healy, and Mr. W. Corcoran, District Trustees; Mr. Thomas Lawlor, District Secretary; Mr. P. J. Shanley, Mr. Wilson, Mr. Doyle, &c. There were several flat races for prizes varying from 5s. to 15s., which were distributed by Mr. Healy and Mr. Dowling. After the sports had concluded, the excursionists proceeded homewards by both routes to the Beauparc Station, by the southern bank of the river or by the road, and on arriving at the station – thanks to the excellent arrangements of the Dublin and Drogheda Railway Company, under the immediate direction of their officers, Mr. Browne, Station Master at Amiens-street Terminus, and Mr. Curry, of the locomotive department – were quickly despatched by special trains to Dublin, thus ending a day's pleasure disturbed only by the sad accident already mentioned. It should be stated that a young man named Fred Leland made a praiseworthy effort to save the woman. He stripped off his coat, and jumped into the river, but perhaps fearing that he would not be able to reach her, gave up the effort after he had reached the centre of this rather broad stream.

Article published by The Irish Times on Saturday May 25, 1872.

A FATHER SHOOTING HIS SON.

Drogheda, Saturday

Intelligence has been received here of a fearful occurrence which took place last night near Beauparc. A lock-keeper on the Meath canal, named Luke Maguire, in a family squabble, shot his own son, John Maguire aged 22 and he died in half an hour. The young man had been a telegraph clerk, but latterly lived *with his father. The mother was drowned on the occasion of a Foresters' fete at Slane.*

FURTHER PARTICULARS

An investigation by the police, assisted by the resident magistrate, was held today, into the tragedy of last night. Considerable coolness, I understand, was manifested in the unfortunate business. The gun was loaded with a heavy charge of large shot, and alleged to have been aimed at the young man's breast. He, however, seeing the design of his father, is stated to have knocked down the muzzle of the piece, on which he received charge in the groin. The occurrence took place at ten o'clock pm. and by midnight the young man was a corpse. Maguire was taken into custody. For some time back, more especially since the drowning of his wife, Maguire appears to have not lived happily with his family, his violent habits, and frequent intemperance, causing much unpleasantness. He had lost the position of lock-keeper on the Boyne Navigation Canal, which was given to the deceased's son. The result of the investigation was that a warrant was made out for the committal of the prisoner to the county goal at Trim. A coroner's jury was empaneled, who returned a verdict that the deceased died of a gunshot wound inflicted by his father.

Article published by The Nenagh Guardian on 14 January, 1874

I listened with interest when Amanda read the above articles out loud to me, and was surprised to hear how Mrs. Maguire's drowning was reported alongside the frivolities of the fete. In a small, isolated community, all this would have been big news and I wonder what part my grandparents played, if any? Did they go and watch the sports at Slane Castle? Did they comfort their neighbour Luke following the death of his wife? Was Mrs. Maguire my grandmother's friend? Did my grandparents realise, as the second newspaper articles suggests, that Luke wasn't coping very well following her death? Some 27 years later, the 1901 census shows Catherine Maguire, presumably Luke's daughter, as the resident lock-keeper and despite other members of my family moving into the house where this happened several years later, we still always referred to it as Maguire's Lock. The newspaper article reporting the drowning of poor old Tommy Grace back in 1919, confirms this and I always found it strange that two tragic deaths occurred in the very same place, albeit 45 years apart.

4. **Matthew Reilly b.1843 (not confirmed)** was the fourth child of William and Mary Reilly and third brother to travel to America, joining James and William some years later he apparently left home with all his possessions in a tin suitcase and worked his way to America on a passenger ship. On documentation that I have found, he tends to spell his surname as Riley and he is the 'uncle' that I have found out least about. My information is that he married a Mary Farren and had four children, John (which, along with William, seems to be the most popular names in this family), Ellen, Margaret and Mary. Descendants of this family seem to be still located in Cleveland, Ohio and again, contact has been made with descendants through social media. Not much is known about Matthew at all, he worked for the Cleveland & Pittsburgh Railroad Company with his brothers, a fresh start for all of them, many, many miles away from Ireland, Slane and the River Boyne, the land of their birth. Matthew's granddaughter Helen Gafney Lawlor (Nellie) provided some

information via Mary Nemec about Matthew and also believes that Matthew had two sisters, Margaret and Mary Reilly who remained in Ireland.

5. **Mary Reilly b 1845 (Not confirmed)** was a sister of James, William, John and Matthew. She was married to a man called John McGee who died in Ireland leaving her with a small family - the names Maggie, Mary and Henry have been suggested. According to Nellie Lawlor (Matthew's granddaughter), soon after John McGee died, Matthew sent for Mary's children who travelled out to America to seek a better life. Mary's daughter, Maggie McGee married Joseph Minnick, lived in Elyria, Ohio and had six children, Charles, Anna, Eva, Bernard, Frank and Helen whilst Mary McGee married John Kinney and had James, Helen, John, William, Mary, Marcella, Margaret, Harry, Alice and Maxine. I wonder what happened to them all?

6. **Margaret Reilly** - no information.

Paternal Grandparents of John Patrick Reilly

John Reilly	m.	Elizabeth (Eliza) O'Neil
b. 1841		b. 1851
d. 28.1.1905		d. 3.4.1928

Children of John and Eliza Reilly (neé O'Neil)

Although reputed to have had 22 children, I can only name 16. As I was unable to trace names in the parish register when I was kindly given permission to search through them on one occasion, I can only presume that many children died prematurely and that details were not registered or that perhaps they just didn't have as many children as first thought!

1. William Reilly was born on **18.7.1873** in Darlington England, he was raised in Slane, Ireland and he worked in Spicer's bakers' shop in Navan before he emigrated to America. Firstborn son and likely named after his paternal grandfather (William Reilly d1848). Matthew Reilly, his uncle, wrote to him, as he had done to Maggie and Mary McGee, and suggested he too join the family in America as work was plentiful. He too settled in Cleveland, Ohio. His application for American citizenship shows that he first arrived in the United States on 24.10.1889. He married Bridgette Moore and had four children, Florence, Elizabeth, Frances Colette and William. He didn't talk much about his family in Ireland and when he died in 1971, his daughter Florence found a letter from his younger brother Harry in his bureau and she wrote to him to advise him of his brother's death. She sent Harry two memorial cards for

William and Brigette Reilly, that Harry subsequently passed on to me.

2. Mary Reilly. There is a Mary Reilly named on the family headstone at Monknewton Cemetery, who died on 17.8.1916, aged 42. Little else is known about her but as this places her birth in **1874**, it is assumed especially as she is buried in the family plot, that she is the second child of John and Elizabeth Reilly. Firstborn daughter and likely named after her paternal grandmother (Mary Reilly d1849). She is also potentially the mother of Mary Broome, the grand-daughter listed on the 1911 census living with Eliza Reilly in Cruicetown. If she was the mother she would have been 25 when Mary Broome was born in England. Did Mary Reilly travel to England for work like her younger sisters, did she marry or get pregnant and bring the child home to her parents at some point? Was she poorly, why did she die so young? Despite searches in both Ireland and the UK, I have not managed to trace a death certificate for her.

3. Mathew Reilly was born on **17.3.1878.** Another family name and likely named after one of his uncles, Mathew lived and worked around Painstown all his life. He married Catherine Lynch when he was 33 but they did not have any children. He died on 18.12.1925, two and half years before his wife.

4. James Reilly was born on **26.10.1879**. He travelled to America to see his older brother William as well as his uncles who all worked on the railroad in Cleveland, Ohio. William found him a job in the railway offices but after a brief time spent working in administration he returned home to Ireland as America was not for him. He later went to work in England, spending some time working and living around Liverpool docks before settling in St. Helens, where he sought employment in the coal mines. He married Catherine Webster whose first husband Harry Webster had been killed in World War 1. James and Catherine had four children, Sheila, Gerard, Brian and Kevin. Sheila died as an infant and James died in 1946. It was this family that I lived with when I first came to England and Kevin was not only my cousin but he also became my best friend.

5. Catherine (Kate/Kathleen) Reilly is also named on the gravestone in Monknewton cemetery. She was born on **20.7.1881** and died on 2.5.1907 when she was only 25 years old. I am not sure when Kathleen first left for England, but when she was 18 she had a daughter Violet who was born in Caterham, Surrey on 17.3.1899. Kathleen must have returned to Ireland with her baby as Violet was raised by my grandparents, John and Eliza, as one of their own children. Even my father Richard and many of my aunts and uncles believed Violet to be a sister when she was in fact a niece. At the age of 20, Kathleen was back in England and on the 1901 UK census she is working as a domestic cook for William Nicolas and his family in Maidstone Kent. How long she remains with the family is not known but six years later her death is recorded in Cruicetown on 2.5.1907.

 Violet, Kathleen's illegitimate daughter, eventually became a nurse and travelled to England, spending some time with my Uncle Harry and his family in Thatto Heath, St. Helens. Harry still believed Violet to be his sister. I established that in 1922 she was however in Caterham as she too had an illegitimate daughter, called Kathleen, whose

birth is recorded there. Young Kathleen was brought up by Annie Coomber (neé Reilly), her mother's younger sister, who was living in Bognor Regis. Violet arrived unannounced on Annie's doorstep and promised to pay 10/- a week for the upkeep of her child if Annie would take the baby. Annie agreed but only ever saw one payment of 10/-. Violet eventually emigrated in 1928 after writing to my father's eldest brother William in Cleveland Ohio who welcomed her over. After sending off for her travel tickets she waited anxiously for them to arrive but the postman in Slane Village was notoriously lazy and refused to walk down the lane to the family house until he had several letters in hand. By the time he delivered the tickets, Violet had missed her boat and was furious. She is listed as a third class traveller on 'The Duchess of Bedford' which was scheduled to arrive in Quebec on 2.8.1928 and her first port of call is recorded as the Women's Hostel of Montreal. To extract her revenge and before embarking on this voyage she went into Navan and ordered a daily newspaper to be delivered to the house down on the river side so the postman had to take a long walk down the lane every morning to deliver the paper. Sweet! Violet died a young woman in America in 1931 after a cerebral embolism and I wonder if young Kathleen was ever told of her true parentage.

6. John (Jack) Reilly or 'Uncle Jack' was my Godfather. He was born on **8.1.1883** and moved to England where he joined the Metropolitan Police on 10.9.1906 as PC481. He served with the police for 17 years before resigning on 9.9.1923. He married Mary Finnegan, an Irish girl who was five years younger than him in St. Francis'

Church, Notting Hill, London and I was told that she ran away from home to England to be with him against her family's wishes. They lived in Caulsden Common in South London for many years and latterly St. Helens Gardens, North Kensington before returning to live in Fennor, a short distance from my home in Cruicetown. They never had any children of their own but they brought up Jack Reilly, the son of John's brother, Joseph Reilly and his wife Molly Morris, before young Jack left for England at 16 years of age to be with his father. John and Mary also brought up two other children - Jack and Eileen Power, who I presumed to be relatives of my Aunty Mary. John is buried in Stackallan Cemetery off French Lane, whilst Mary is buried up on the Hill of Slane - I never liked the thought of them being separated. I don't think either of them have a headstone.

7. Margaret (Maggie) Reilly This is one of my aunties that I know very little about. She was born on **5.5.1884** and left home to work in service, settling in Bognor Regis, England. She returned to Ireland with a son Thomas Grace at some point and although she always maintained that she was married, none of the family believed her. It was her son Thomas that died in Dooner's Lock and is the subject of the inquest of 1919. The newspaper states that Margaret was already dead by the time the accident happened and as the boy's father was in the army, my grandparents were raising him.

8. Annie Reilly was born **5.5.1887**. She appears on the 1901 Irish Census as a 14 year old scholar and is living at Castlefin Lockhouse with my father and grandparents. She later travelled to England and worked 'in service' in Caterham and this is where her first child Agnes was born in 1908. Shortly after the birth

187

of Agnes, Annie was hospitalised with an embolism which resulted in her losing an eye. The sister she was staying with (presumably Maggie as Kate wasn't in a position to dictate, having found herself in similar circumastances) insisted on Agnes's birth certificate being annotated as illegitimate and on the 1911 census sadly both Annie and Agnes are recored as being in Godstone Union Workhouse in Bletchingley. After a short amount of time Agnes was sent back to Ireland and was looked after by one of Annie's sisters (by all accounts a teacher although I do not know who this was), where she lived until the outbreak of the First World War. Annie eventually sent for her and so she was taken back to England to be with her mother, who by that time was in Felpham near Bognor, married to a George Coomber and with another child called Florence. Sometime around 1922, Violet turned up at Annie's with her daughter Kathleen and Annie agreed to look after the child despite her husband George not being best pleased. In 1928 Annie lost the sight in her remaining eye and was registered blind, just like me! Annie died of a brain tumour in 1948 and she is buried in Felpham Churchyard.

9. Alice Reilly was the aunt I knew best of all. She was born on **24.2.1889** and she lived further along the River Boyne in the next lock house, known as Carridexter Lock so our early lives were very much intertwined. On the 1901 Irish census she is living at Carrickdexter Lock with her brother John (Jack), sister Maggie and brother Harry and ten years later she is still living on the banks of the Boyne, but as part of a much larger family. In 1909, when only 20, she married a widower called Edward Reilly, who we all called 'Sailor Reilly' and as a consequence she never changed her name. Edward already had four children when he married my Aunty Alice - Madeleine, Edwards's eldest daughter was in fact only eight years her junior, then there was Cissie, Margaret and Edward (junior). It must have been quite a culture shock. She went on to have eight children of her own however with Edward Reilly - John, Sheila, Lily, Winnie, Willie, Oliver, Kitty and Phyllis and as a young man, Rita and I would enjoy many family days out with her eldest son John, his wife Kathleen and their children. John and Kathleen eventually had ten children and just like me, they lost a child tragically in a motor accident when only a young man. John, Kathleen and their son John are buried in the small churchyard at the back of Rushwee Chapel and I visit their grave every time I return home. Alice's son Willie was responsible for getting me the job in Gerrity's furniture factory in Navan and it is always a great joy to see all my cousins from this family whenever I am home. Phyllis, now married to Ultan Dunne has also always remained one of my closest friends over the years. My Uncle Edward died in 1934 when he was 63, he was a lot older than Alice and as a consequence she lived almost 40 years as a widow. She died in 1973, aged 84 and she is buried up on The Hill of Slane.

10. Henry (Harry) Reilly was a colourful character and as he lived in St. Helens for many years, I remained close to him. He was born on **27.7.1890** and after apparently deserting from the Irish Army, he went to live with his brother James in St. Helens, England. The local police however, made it known to James that they knew Harry was staying with him and discreetly suggested to him that he 'move on'. Harry did, he moved to London to stay with his brother John who was the Metropolitan Policeman. I can only think that Harry liked living dangerously and by all accounts he would walk with John on his beat, making out he was a detective!! Harry married Nellie (Eleanor Thomas) who was Welsh and not a Catholic and they had four children, Mary (Blodwyn), Gwillam, Joan, and John. I seem to recall that Blodwyn was born unexpectedly whilst on holiday in Ireland and my grandmother Eliza Reilly, was not happy that her daughter-in-law Nell, who was dedicated to her own Welsh Chapel upbringing, was not going to give her a traditional Irish name or baptise her a Roman Catholic. Without Nell's permission, my grandmother took Blodwyn and had her christened Mary - hence her name. Despite this, she was always known as Blodwyn so perhaps Nell got her own way in the end! I was friendly with all of this family and became known to them as 'Jonny Irish'. When I married Rita in 1953, Harry and his family came to my wedding, with Harry standing in for my father. After Nell died, Harry married Elsie and lived for a time in Rhyl and I often visited him there in his little bungalow. After Elsie died, he returned to live in St. Helens with his daughter Joan, who had never married. He died in 1973 and is buried in St. Helens Cemetery. Sadly I last saw any of this family at Blodwyn's funeral, when Amanda took me over to the Service of Remembrance at Boardmans Lane Methodist Church on 23.9.2010. I enjoyed chatting to Rena, my cousin John's wife and with family that were always familiar to me.

11. Thomas (Tom) Reilly lived and worked at Beauparc House all his life and he could often be seen rowing across the River Boyne to visit my family on the north bank. Most of the lock cottages had a small boat house and there was always a small boat available for friends and family to use. He was born in **1893** and despite his proximity to our family when I was a boy, I don't really know a lot about him. He married Elizabeth Hoey who was a tall and very thin woman which always amused me because he was a short and chubby man and I remember him being very fussy. As a boy I would stand mesmerised as I watched him brush his hair with two brushes at the same time, his arms going round and round at the side of his head like feet peddling a bike. He had eight children with Elizabeth, Lily, John, Elizabeth, Nancy, Kathleen, Mary, Michael and Annie. (Jack) died in his early twenties and I seem to think it would have been around 1943 as I remember going to the funeral with my father and although I'm not sure, I also think he may be buried in Monknewton Cemetery. Elizabeth also died in her 20s, as did Nancy. I'm not sure what happened to Kathleen but I know that Annie only died in 2005 and she was 83, a good age. Michael I believe is still alive. Tom and Elizabeth are both buried in Beauparc, Elizabeth died on 27.1.1981 when she was 81 and Tom died on 24.5.1984 aged 91.

12 & 13 Bridgette and Elizabeth were twins born on **3.2.1894** but were quite poorly children. They died when they were both about eight months old. I only became aware of them through searching the Parish Records many, many years ago and even my mother who knew a lot about this generation of the family, did not know any more about them.

14 Joseph (Joe) Reilly was born in **1895** and found work on a farm which entitled him to live in a cottage provided by his employer. Unfortunately an old woman lived in the cottage and she initially refused to vacate the premises for Joseph, his wife Molly and their children, John (Jack), William and May. After the farmer intervened she was left with no choice and as she reluctantly left, she spat and snarled and wished 'three curses' on Joseph for forcing her to move on. Tragedy soon fell on him as his son William was kicked by Finnegan's pony when he was about seven years old and died as a result. Five years later, when May was 11, her nightdress caught fire when she was staying at my Uncle Jack and Aunty Mary's house. I remember May very well as she was a little older than me and she had beautiful long hair, but she stretched up to reach for something on the hearth and flames engulfed her. She died from her burns and I remember everyone in the family feeling terribly sad. Soon after these two accidents, Joe's wife Mary died suddenly too - it seems that the old woman's 'three curses' were very effective. Joseph left for England soon after the death of his wife, leaving his eldest son John (Jack) with Aunty Mary and Uncle Jack in Fennor. He travelled to see his sister Annie who was living in Bognor but just before he left he went to Navan and ordered a new suit and new shoes for himself. Nothing untoward about that except that he charged them to my father, who was absolutely furious. After he was settled in England, he sent for his son Jack who travelled over to England on his own when he was 16 - some time around 1935. Neither ever returned to Ireland, not even for a visit. I met up with both my Uncle Joe and cousin Jack around 1976 and Jack spoke of his journey to England, explaining that he set off for Dublin on his own where someone met him to take him to the ferry to Liverpool. Someone else met him at Liverpool and put him on the train to London, where he met a third stranger who put him on the train to Bognor. When he arrived at the station, although relieved to see his father, he was cold and hungry and remembered feeling grateful that his long journey had finally come to an end!

Joseph married a second time in England to a lovely lady called Frances and he had six more children, Michael John who spent 22 years in the Army before working as a prison officer in Winchester,

Nolan who lived in Littlehampton, Tom, Pat and then Anne and Susan who were twins. He was also a despatch rider in the army during the Second World War but was badly injured after getting blown up and as a consequence he received a full Army Pension.

15. Richard (Dick) Reilly was born on **3.7.1900**, he was my father. He was born in Castlefin Lock house and although he wasn't the youngest of the family, he was the last to leave home. Before he was even five years old his father had died and I can only imagine that life must have been rather difficult for him. When he was 14 years old there was an inspection of the derelict canal and a report produced for Meath County Council, by the engineer P. J. Kennedy. Presumably this helped decide the future of the canal, whether it should be kept open to traffic and whether it would survive as a paying concern or not. Regardless of why it was produced, the detail of that report has provided me with a greater understanding of life down on the riverbank in the years surrounding my father's childhood. I have reproduced extracts from that report below for information: -

1914 EXHAUSTIVE REPORT (Extracts)
By Mr. P. J Kennedy of Rathcore
To Meath County Council

"Banks. The canals are, on the whole, well maintained; only in a few places did I see where banks required attention, and then damage was principally due to cattle being allowed to break down rib when coming to drink, and owners should be called on to make good the rib and bank."

"Rampart Walls. Some of the rampart walls have been allowed to get overgrown with ash plants and small trees (especially the wall above Riley's lock) and lock-keepers should be instructed to have all these cut away, otherwise the walls will require to be rebuilt in the course of a few years."

"Locks. The locks, without exception, are in good order, very little repairs to masonry being necessary, and to prevent them falling into bad condition, the lock-keepers should keep grass from growing in the joints of the walls or above the lock. In a couple of cases the lock-keeper might be supplied with a bag of cement to point the upper course of the lock."

"Lock-Houses. The lock-houses were in fairly good condition but require some attention! I may mention a few items: - Riley's lock: chimney is bad and no ridge tiles are on the roof. Carrickdexter: slating and chimney requires repairs. Rosnaree: roof leaking at west side. Cruicetown house is empty and bad; and Bective house is let for fishing lodge."

"Lock gates. If the navigation is to be maintained, it is absolutely necessary that the lock-gates be put into

good, safe working order, and I paid special attention to the lock gates in my examination."

"*Lock-keepers.* Lock-keepers all state they have not received any wages for nearly two years. As these all have the grazing of the banks, they should be made see after the small slips and such damage as is caused by cattle; and also an arrangement might be made as regards their scraping and painting the lock gates and of whitewashing and painting lock-houses."

"*Repairs and Maintenance.* To work this canal properly, the gates and canals should be well maintained, and I consider a lock-carpenter should be employed as a working foreman and inspector, he should he held responsible for keeping the navigation in order; if the small repairs were attended to at once much heavy expenditure would be avoided; such a man might be appointed as a lock-keeper, and thus be provided with a house convenient to his duties, and as part wages, during the winter months he could build a set of gates as may be required form time to time. I would also recommend that all lock-gates be painted once a year, or even coated with black varnish as I noticed that some new work had been neglected as regards to this, and so must only be expected to rapidly deteriorate in consequence. I do not see why this navigation should not be self-supporting; should be well able to keep at least six boats going, and if these were worked to the best advantage – either by traders or a carrying concern – I fail to see why it should not pay its way.

Navan lock – Deep gate mitre and sheeting required.

Footboards and handrails repaired. Cost about … £35.

Ruxton Lock – Gates in good order.

Rowley's – Swing beam to be fitted and deep gates to be re-sheeted … £12

Bective Lock – Swing beam to be fitted, handrails to be replaced … £4

Thompson's Lock – Two loggerheads, D.G. and stone in wall of lock, handrails etc … £7

Stackallan Lock – Handrail B.G. broken, logger head, D.G. … £3

Deerpark Lock – Handrails and racks … £2

Riley's Lock – Do. … £2

Carrickdexter – Do. And sheeting … £5

Castle Lock – Footboards and runner plate … £6

Slane Lock – Fair order.

Rosnaree Lock – Good.

Broe Lock – Upper deep gate to be repaired and new breast gates required … £120

Broke Lock – Lower – logger head footboards and new square for broken rail … £10

Staleen Lock – Upper – good.

Staleen Lock – Lower – good.

Oldbridge Lock – Upper – New swing beam required for breast gate, etc £5

Oldbridge Lock – Lower – New deep gates £120.

Sluice gears require a general overhauling, at say … £40.

"Motors. There is certainly an opening for a motor barge service and in the summer or tourist season, if a regular service was maintained, provision might be made for the conveying of passengers along what might be termed 'the most picturesque and historic valley and river in Ireland' and so in this way also assist the revenue of the canal. Motor barges would keep the canal free from weeds, and it would thus be suitable for small pleasure craft and on holidays and Sundays, the motors could be utilized for passenger trips."

"... I can now confirm the toll on boats using the canal and belonging to persons other than the Company only £1 per trip ... "

"... we got from the Liquidator the enclosed list of lock-keepers showing their wages and the arrears due to them ... we inspected the agreements under which the lock-keepers held their houses. Five of them were in as caretakers at 1d per week under signed Agreements and the remainder were in under Agreements as servants of the Company ... The duties of the lock-keepers were not definitely set out, but they would naturally be to attend to the locks and take care of them under Lock Houses."

"List of lock-keepers showing arrears of wages to 30th April 1913, claimed by them form the Liquidator and still unpaid at 31st March 1914.

Quarterly Wages

		£	s	d
1	A. Dowdall, Farganstown, Navan	0	10	6
2	John Murphy, Ardmulchan, Navan	0	7	0
3	Mrs. John Murphy, Stackallan, Navan	0	10	6
4	John Englishby, Deepark, Stackallan	0	10	6

5	Edward Reilly, Carrickdexter, Slane	1	3	6
6	Mrs. Eliza Reilly, Cruicetown, Stackallan	1	0	0
7	Mrs. Eliza Reilly, CastleFin, Cruicetown	1	5	3

Monthly Wages

8	Mrs. J. Givern, Fennor, Slane	1	5	0
9	Owen Morgan, Rosnaree, Slane	0	12	0
10	Mrs. A. Callan, Broe Locks, Slane	0	12	2
11	Christopher Neary, Staleen, Drogheda	0	7	4
12	Reps. P. Tiernan Deceased, Oldbridge	2	2	0

After reading the report I felt sad that the old house was in need of attention. I can only imagine that since being made a widow, home maintenance was more difficult for my grandmother. My father was only a boy in 1914, his older siblings would have full time jobs and possibly be living elsewhere and I would love to think that the repairs to the canal and the lock-keeper's cottages were made. Even more importantly though I hope my grandmother received the arrears she was owed. I wonder did those living along the canal, my father and grandmother included, realise that the situation was irrevocably changing. It would have been a simple existence, even more so than my own and with a young family and no support from a husband, I wonder how on earth my grandmother managed.

I never heard my father complain about his childhood. I guess like me he played in the woods with his brothers and sisters, trundled to a school somewhere for a short while before finding work. He eventually worked up at Stackallan House and earned 18/- per week and an extra 2/- for working on a Sunday – and as a young man, he was allegedly, the best paid on the estate. Stackallan House was taken over by the Irish Military during the war but in the main 275 acres were rented out as grazing land and my father was responsible for managing this. In addition to working up at the estate, he also owned his own cows, many young calves as well as pigs which he fattened up and killed for bacon. Together he and my mother had a good-sized small holding, which kept them both very busy. He married Catherine (Kitty) Harding and together they had seven children of which I am the eldest. My sister Betty comes next, followed closely by, Delia, then Liam, who was always told he was a twin, Maureen, Patsy and finally Seamus who is 20 years younger than me. When the phone call came through to tell me that my father was sick, I travelled home immediately. It was a difficult journey that I made on my own, I knew this would be my final goodbye but I was thankful that I had chance to see him, talk to him and hold his hand before he died in hospital on 20th October 1971. He was a good man, he taught me values and ethics, he let me live the life I wanted. I hope I made him proud.

16. Christopher (Christy) Reilly - last but not least. Born on

29.12.1901, he married Josephine Coogan on 17.12.1924 and had five children, Anna, Sean (John), Elizabeth (Betty), Margaret (Peggy) and Anthony. Like my Uncle Harry, Christie had an eventful life and even had a spell in the Irish National Army. He told me that he joined up in May 1922 and each time I went home, I would often take myself off to spend time with him. I loved hearing about his exploits and stories from when he was a young man, his life seemed so exciting to me and consequently he remained a firm favourite of mine. He lived up at Donore for a while and eventually in Beauparc, not far from my sister Betty. A trip home would not have been complete without a visit to see him.

With regard to my paternal grandmother, Elizabeth O'Neil. There are no records of her birth but she is believed to have been born in either Rossan or Rosnaree - both places have been suggested. She was allegedly brought up by 'The Flemmings' who managed The Conyngham Arms, Hotel in Slane. An extensive search of records has not unearthed anything of value.

Maternal Ancestors of John Patrick Reilly

My Grandmother Alice Harding (neé Waters), my mother Kitty as a child, my grandfather Patrick holding my Uncle John c 1910 outside the house at McGruder's Cross

I have always concentrated my family research efforts on my father's side of the family and I think this is mainly because, from being a young boy, I heard tales of travel, adventure and far away places associated with many of my Reilly relatives. My mother's family always lived around the locality, and of course, my mother's parents were the only grandparents known to me. My mother was born Catherine Harding and she was the eldest of 12 children and something I always found amusing was that I was two years older than her youngest brother - my Uncle Brendan! The house she was born into was up at McGruder's Cross, in the locality know as Johnstown, it was where my grandfather Harding was born and family still live in the same house today, albeit on a grander scale.

Maternal Great Grandparents of John Patrick Reilly

John Waters	m.	Mary Flanagan
b. 1859		b. 1866
d. 1899		d. 1943

My great-grandfather John Waters was from Mornington on the coast, just east of Drogheda and he was a horse trainer. He died in hospital from peritonitis on 4th September 1899, as a result of injuries received by a fall from a horse he was riding on 27th August. At the time of his death, he was just 40 years old, the family were living in Painstown and he left a young wife aged 33 and seven children all under the age of 11, Peter, Alice (my grandmother), Jack, Maggie, Mary, Patrick and Bridgette (Dolly). His wife Mary Flanagan had been an only child as her mother had died immediately following her birth, although Mary's father did remarry and she had seven half-brothers as a consequence. I suspect that my grandmother Alice, being the eldest daughter and despite being only ten years old, would have had to take on a lot of household responsibility following the death of her father.

Maternal Grandparents of John Patrick Reilly

Patrick Harding	m.	Alice Waters
b. 1880		b. 1890
d. 1967		d. 1980

Alice married my grandfather Patrick Harding on 15th February 1908, a week after her 18th birthday. He was the only son of John Harding and Catherine Murtagh but he had five sisters, Catherine, Annie, Mary, Rose, and Ellie. My mother Catherine (Kitty) was born nine months later on 26th November 1908. In quick succession, my grandmother then had John, Maureen. Patrick, Peter, Rose,

Alacoque, Anne, Nancy, Gerald, Erc and Brendan. Every trip I made home, I always found time to visit the little house at McGruder's Cross, the house I have fond memories of visiting as a boy and where I worked with my grandfather Patrick in his garden. My grandparents are buried in Stackallan cemetery, which was sadly very overgrown on my last visit home.

The Harding Family

Left to right: Brendan, Eric, Nancy, John, Rose, Grandfather (Patrick), Peter, Catherine (Kitty, my mother), Grandmother (Alice), Alacoque, Patrick, Maureen and Gerald

Always time for brothers and sisters –
clockwise from top left, with Betty,
Delia, Liam, Seamus, Patsy and
Maureen.

John and Rita in their garden c1998

Slane Bridge